Neil Ansell was an award-winning television journalist with the BBC and a long standing newspaper journalist. He is the author of *Deep Country*, *Deer Island* and *The Last Wilderness* which was shortlisted for the 2018 Wainwright Golden Beer and Highland Book Prizes. He has two daughters and lives in Brighton.

Praise for Neil Ansell's writing:

'A beautiful evocation of life in a forest and a powerful reminder of the interconnected fate of all wild things, including ourselves' Raynor Winn

'Like taking a refreshing and eye-opening walk in the open air with the most interesting, observant and companionable of guides. In *The Circling Sky* Neil Ansell reveals the remarkableness of the relatively unexotic New Forest, moving deftly from personal reflection to beautiful nature writing, to a crucial, timely argument about the history and importance of common land' Naomi Ishiguro

'Neil Ansell's series of walks in the New Forest through the course of a year coalesce into a skilful exploration of memory, childhood, and how certain landscapes can become an integral part of your life. Ansell is a gifted naturalist, sensitive, inquisitive, at times justly enraged, invariably joyful . . . a wonderful tribute to a unique and precious place' James Macdonald Lockhart

'Reads like a vivid and subtle nature programme for your mind's eye. Its New Forest setting is a world within a world; a fragile Eden with an utterly astonishing cast of birds; a unique harbour to an array of species both familiar and unexpected, and a complex, sometimes dark human history. I finished this book sharing its author's desire to look closer, to "walk in peace", and – as he puts it – to "camp without camping", and simply fall asleep beneath a tree' Damian Le Bas

'Neil Ansell takes us on a thoughtful journey through the fabulous New Forest. He combines evocative description with an accurate naturalist's eye, in the best tradition of modern British nature writing' Jeremy Purseglove

'His anecdotes gleam' *TLS*

'An immersive delving into the delights of the New Forest. Neil Ansell writes with such warmth and such wonder on the wild – with vital eyes and mind he senses the essence of the world around him, tucked down in the landscape to observe better the life of the natural world' Dr James Canton

'Ansell's beautiful memoir of his walks through the Scottish wilderness makes the case for being truly a part of nature rather than outside of it' *Observer*

'[A] captivating memoir . . . vivid as photographs, yet sketched with something more profound than simple reportage. Beneath the measured, knowledgeable, unfussy voice is a meaningful, and even important record: not just of a changing landscape, but of a man such places have shaped' *The Herald*

'Beautiful . . . a testimony to reticent courage' *Daily Mail*

'Lyrical, thought-provoking' *Scotsman*

'Neil Ansell is a genuine creature of the wild. His knowledge of remote places, and his love for them, come from deep and sustained immersion. He writes in prose which is entirely right for its subject – unshowy, level-headed, quietly surprising. *The Last Wilderness* is a wonderful experience which tingles with all the sensations of being out on the hill, in all weathers, alone' Philip Marsden

'Ansell has the rare skill of combining vividly the intimacy of detail and the astonishing grandeur of this North West coastline of Scotland. Through his keen eyes we look again at the familiar with a sense of wondrous revelation' Madeleine Bunting

'Beautifully charts the challenges and solaces of being alone and part of nature' *Bookseller*

NEIL ANSELL

The Circling Sky

ON NATURE AND BELONGING
IN AN ANCIENT FOREST

TINDER
PRESS

First published in Great Britain in 2021 by Tinder Press
An imprint of HEADLINE PUBLISHING GROUP

First published in this paperback edition in 2022 by Tinder Press
An imprint of HEADLINE PUBLISHING GROUP

Cataloguing in Publication Data is available from the British Library

ISBN 978 1 4722 7237 9

Typeset in Scala by Avon DataSet Ltd, Alcester, Warwickshire

Printed and bound in Great Britain by Clays Ltd, Elcograf S.p.A.

Headline's policy is to use papers that are natural, renewable and recyclable
products and made from wood grown in well-managed forests and other
controlled sources. The logging and manufacturing processes are expected
to conform to the environmental regulations of the country of origin.

HEADLINE PUBLISHING GROUP
An Hachette UK Company
Carmelite House
50 Victoria Embankment
London EC4Y 0DZ

www.tinderpress.co.uk
www.headline.co.uk
www.hachette.co.uk

Contents

PREFACE

Root and Branch

April 2020

I t is perhaps wise to wait until a book is finished before writing the introduction. Only then do you really have much idea of just what it is that you are introducing. Books have a tendency to take their own routes to the final destination, and lead you down unexpected byways. This is notoriously true of fiction, but it can also be the case with memoir, especially memoir that is written while the events it describes are still unfolding. Life is full of surprises, and the future is not easy to anticipate.

I write these introductory notes from a time of lockdown, when the future seems more unpredictable than ever. Just a few short months ago, our current situation would have seemed almost beyond our imaginings. It is striking how, in these uncertain times, people seem to have turned to nature to find solace. It helps, perhaps, that it is springtime, and the world is filled with new life; a kind of rebirth. People turn their focus to every new marker: the first spring flowers, the first butterflies and bumblebees, the return of our migrant birds, one by one by one. They seem to give us a measure of reassurance that the world is still turning.

Living on a very short leash perhaps urges us towards a greater appreciation of what we have, of what is on our doorstep. In my case, living without a garden, my local patch is a small unlovely area of chalk down and urban wasteland overlooking the sea. It is scrubby with sycamore and bramble and ivy, it is litter-strewn, criss-crossed by trails made by dog-walkers, full of dens and rope swings left by children, and with abandoned camps made by homeless people among the undergrowth. It is surrounded by council estates on all sides, but for now it is all I have. Hitherto I have largely ignored it, but now I find myself taking the short walk there almost every day. Last week I stood on the hilltop and watched my first swallows of the year heading north, just flown in from across the sea, coming to the end of a journey that had taken them halfway across the world. Today, a buzzard was circling overhead, and the bluebells and a patchwork of other wild flowers were in bloom. A robin pinged onto a nearby twig, its beak stuffed full of insects, then disappeared into the tangle of ivy at the foot of a twisted ash tree. It is raising young early this year, encouraged by the fine weather. Among the spring butterflies were the very first holly blues, newly emerged.

I can only hope that when we finally, hopefully, also emerge and get back to a semblance of normality, blinking into the light, we will do so with a greater appreciation of just how much the natural world means to us, and with a renewed sense of the urgency of keeping it safe.

Much of my previous writing has been set in the wilder reaches of the British Isles, or even further afield, but my childhood was spent on the south coast of England, in Hampshire, and it was here that I learned most of what I know now as a naturalist. It felt that the time was long overdue that I finally revisited the places that formed me, for better and for worse. My love of nature was forged on those chalk downs, on those coastal marshes, and perhaps most of all in the New Forest, which always seemed to me like a kind of promised land, a place where I could see so many things that I never saw around my home, and where one side of my family had their roots. In the decades since I left the place of my birth, I had seldom had cause to return. I tell myself that it was not that I was running away, but that I was running towards; moving ever onwards, in search of greater adventures. But perhaps when we tell ourselves the story of our lives, we always try to put the most positive spin possible upon it, and imagine our lives as a kind of hero's journey in which we are destined for greatness, when the reality is that the course of our lives is most likely determined by random events over which we have little or no control, and by bad choices that we retrospectively justify to ourselves as having been inevitable.

Having decided that it was time to return to the places I remembered from my childhood, it was the New Forest that called to me most insistently, in a voice I could no longer ignore. I would have to go back repeatedly, I determined, for at least a year. Any less than a year would seem like a snapshot, I thought. You need to see a place in every season, every weather, in order to begin to get its true measure. It was time to walk those woods again at last, even if I would perhaps find them haunted by the ghost of my childhood self. It was time to examine the familiar with the same enthusiasm that I have always sought out the new. And perhaps it would give me some insight into some of those questions that hover, unanswered, in the backs of our minds. Who am I? What am I doing here? Where do I belong?

The New Forest has only been a national park since 2005, but has not substantially changed since the days when I first explored it in the sixties and seventies. In fact, it has not essentially changed in a thousand years or more; that is the whole point of it. Its unique blend of ancient woodland, of lowland heath and valley mire has maintained, through what is almost a fluke of history, a continuity that is missing almost everywhere else in the country. This patchwork landscape extends over more than two hundred square miles, and is still home to many plants and animals with specialised habitat requirements, some of which have survived almost no-where else in Britain. It continues to be largely managed as a working common, a way of living with the land that has died out, or more accurately been killed off, just about everywhere else in the country.

This landscape may look wild and beautiful, but in

truth I would never be far from other people; the national park supposedly absorbs some fifteen million visitors every year, although many will stay in the vicinity of the villages and car parks at established beauty spots. I have dedicated much of my life to seeking out some of the wildest and most unpopulated areas of the earth, so it would take some adjustment on my part to be so often reminded that I was in a shared space. That said, it is still perhaps possible to lose yourself in these woods. You just need to get away from the roads and the designated cycle paths, step off the beaten track, and perhaps be prepared to get your feet wet. My purpose in coming here now was different, anyway, for it was not so much about trying to isolate myself and constantly break new ground as it was about going back to my beginnings; roots rather than branches.

A few years ago, when my father died, I was clearing out the beachfront bungalow that he had retired to when I came upon three of my childhood diaries buried in a bottom drawer. To be honest, I was surprised that he had kept them. They covered the period from when I was twelve to fifteen, and made me smile to remember just how single-minded I was as a youngster. Home life, school life, friends; all got barely a mention. These were just a backdrop, a frame to the real business of my life, which was wandering alone in the woods, watching and studying the natural world. Perhaps because this was a solitary, private love, it never really became a matter of competition. It wasn't about checklists and milestones. It is a pleasure to see in those diaries that while I might be delighted to come upon something rare or new, I was just as happy recording the comings and goings of the commonplace. The diaries are full of little maps, showing, for example, the flight paths of the local pair of kestrels, or the locations and counts of various orchid species, or where certain birds were nesting that year, and charts of my studies of small mammals caught in live traps; wood mice and yellow-necked mice, and bank voles and field voles. These diaries contain a record of my reading too: from Charles Darwin's *On the Origin of Species* and Gilbert White's *The Natural History of Selborne* to field guides covering just about every class of life on earth, from fossils to ferns, from mosses to mammals. I think it is fair to say that my interest was close to being obsessive and all-encompassing. I can see from these diaries that, over the course of those three years, I visited the New Forest perhaps fifteen times or so in all, whenever I could, including a couple of school camping expeditions.

I wonder just how many budding naturalists were inspired in part by childhood visits to the New Forest. In his book *Wildwood*, Roger Deakin describes the influence of repeated school camping trips here, and how the surveys his schoolmaster conducted developed his interest in botany in particular, and nature more generally. Another naturalist who found his inspiration here was the conservationist Colin Tubbs, author of the definitive works on the natural history and ecology of the forest. He was a Pompey lad like me, born and raised in Portsmouth, and like me too, he would spend his winters watching birds on the marshes in Langstone Harbour and his summers going on trips to the forest. Unlike me, he never left the area, and spent most of his life living and working in the New Forest.

As I grew up I became a little less single-minded in my interests. In the last of those three diaries, while there was no let-up in the daily sightings of birds and animals and the lists of all the nature books that I was poring over, other interests began to show their first signs of intruding on my life: bands seen, records bought, even girls met. I was perhaps inevitably beginning to become more attuned to the social concerns of a normal teenage boy. And then I set out into the world without much of a plan, to just see where it would lead me. It led me to a lot of places, but never back home, at least not for more than a flying visit. But still, whenever I found myself surrounded by nature, I soon discovered that the boy in the woods was never far away. The decades have passed, and in all those years I have only returned to this forest a scant handful of times. Yet now, after all this time, I feel my past calling me back. As I have become older, I am able to recognise more and more of the person that I have become in those childhood diaries; it is as if I am reverting to type. I want to see what has changed and what has stayed the same, what is lost and gone and what is holding strong; in the forest and in myself.

ONE

Remembrance Day

January 2019

It is a clear, cold January morning in the forest, and I am revisiting my childhood haunts. A chill wind is blowing hard across the heath at Shatterford, setting my eyes streaming, and some of the more sheltered boggy pools are coated with a thin skin of ice. The winter sun glints and sparks from the surface, and I hunker down to shelter from the blast of cold air and give one of these frozen pools some more focused attention. The ice has not formed a clear pane but is wrinkled and patterned with a filigree of frost. It has formed slowly overnight while the temperatures fell, growing incrementally, fractally, until it resembles nothing so much as a fossil bed of petrified ferns. It is beautiful, complex, like a kind of inorganic life. At first the heath seems bereft of birds, but then a pair of hardy stonechats emerge and scold me from the heather tops, a little flash of orange among the dun browns of the winter heath. And then I hear the croaking call of a raven. As is so often the case, I can hear it long before I can see it, so I pause and wait until it soars into view over the treetops.

I never once saw a raven here as a child; could not have done, for they had been persecuted to the point of eradication, and were absent from the entire county for over a century. But in recent years they have begun to return, although they have not been universally welcomed; like birds of prey, the crow family are often treated with suspicion. It feels like a good omen, to see one so soon after my arrival. I don't really believe in omens, but if any bird could be ominous, then it would have to be the raven. So much of my life has been spent among them that it almost feels as though I have brought this bird with me, carried back into my past. For all those years that they were missing, ravens lived on in the forest in name only, in Ravens Nest Inclosure, a wood planted in 1775 to provide oak for shipbuilding. It is good to think that this wood could once again echo to the calls of a real live raven, rather than just the memory of one.

The trail leads me across the heath and into the woods. The trees are bare and last year's leaves and the dried-out husks of beech mast crunch beneath my feet; there is dead wood everywhere, both standing and fallen, much of it riddled with woodpecker holes as if it has been infested with giant woodworm. A few ponies are just visible far off between the tree trunks, sheltering under the scanty cover. I pause to sit on a fallen bough, and although as I arrive the wood seems entirely still the little woodland birds soon begin to materialise around me, and I discover that I am actually surrounded by life. I soon set off again, for it is too cold to stay still, skirting the edge of the woods, passing clear shallow streams that reflect the hard blue sky. Though there are some winter birds that I would particularly like to see, I am careful not to raise my hopes. It is wiser to just go out with eyes wide open, to fully appreciate what is actually there, rather than ending up regretting what is absent.

Out across the heath is a larger, flooded and brilliant blue unfrozen pool backed by a copse of pine and birch trees that are reflected in the waters below, and I am tempted to leave the trail and approach closer, for purely aesthetic reasons, for it strikes me as a spot of particular beauty. And then I see it, perched atop a dead birch right at the water's edge. Pale grey back and long tail, black eye-mask and hooked bill. A great grey shrike.

Only fifty or so of these birds arrive in Britain each winter from their breeding sites in Scandinavia, so the chances of stumbling across one by accident are not great. But they are solitary birds, and establish large winter territories, which may be used year after year, and I knew that this area was one of their favoured sites. My pleasure in coming upon one is not really related to its rarity. It has an elegance, a vitality, about it; the spark of life burns brightly in this bird. It has charisma, though such a quality cannot be entirely intrinsic to the bird itself, but must be related to my perception of it, the thoughts and feelings it evokes in me. I last saw shrikes in the forest in 1971, before I was even a teenager, though that was not this wintering bird but its smaller and more colourful cousin, the red-backed shrike. The red-back is a ferocious predator, sometimes known as the butcher bird for its habit of storing a larder of its prey impaled on the spikes of a thorn bush, but it is barely bigger than a sparrow. Although they were already in steep decline, I had the good fortune to come upon a pair of these beautiful little birds at their nesting site in the straggle of gorse by a winding stream in a valley bottom, somewhere a few miles north-west of here. A year later I returned to the same spot to look for them again, but there was no sign of them. It is possible that this was one of the very last pairs to breed in the forest, for they have not returned since. Occasionally, a pair will turn up somewhere in Britain, but this is not even an annual event, and they are effectively extinct as a British breeding bird. The reasons for birds' rapid contractions or expansions in range, and their sudden population declines, are not always immediately obvious. They may be living their lives on more of a knife-edge than we could ever imagine.

It is not just me who has noticed the great grey shrike on the heath. A buzzard comes wheeling in, flies in tight circles over the copse, and crashes down into a nearby pine. The shrike flushes, taking off across the heath, rising and falling, bounding in flight like a woodpecker, and is lost to view.

I stand at the woodland edge and look out onto the heath. There are some generous thickets of gorse bushes, scattered with bright yellow flowers even now in January, a welcome splash of colour among the winter drabs.

There is a sturdy oak among the dead bracken, its branches twisting in a maze of zigzags, as if it could never quite make up its mind where it was going next, rather like myself. This is characteristic of the oak; in a wood, where it is fighting for the light, it may grow straight and true, but out in the open it will often end up like this, all elbows and knees.

It is an utterly distinctive landscape; in all my travels I have not come upon another place that looked quite like it, although I suppose that could be said of anywhere, if you just look close enough. Still, if you were to blindfold me and drop me anywhere in the New Forest, I suspect I would know instantly where I had landed. A couple of hundred square miles of mostly unenclosed common land, about half of it ancient semi-natural wood pasture grazed by free-roaming cattle and ponies and wild deer, grazing that gives it an unexpected open quality. I am not used to having such long views when I am in a wood. Most of the rest of the forest is lowland heath, a vanishingly rare habitat both nationally and internationally. It looks, if anything, like a kind of temperate savannah. While the vast majority of our lowland heaths have been lost – and by 'lost' I mean destroyed – the little that remains still constitutes about a fifth of the entire world supply. Most of it is dry heathland, but in the valley bottoms are boggy mires filled with sphagnum mosses and sundews and rare flowering plants. These valley mires are even more of a local speciality; according to the National Park authority there are a hundred and twenty of them all told in north-western Europe, and ninety of them are in the New Forest, three quarters of the total. And there are large grassy clearings in the woods, grazed to within an inch of their lives by the ponies that gather there, that look like nothing so much as golf courses and are known as 'lawns'.

It is this patchwork of scarce habitats that makes the place so exceptional, a place of last resort for so many specialised and endangered plants and animals that you are unlikely to come across elsewhere, and some of which are found only here, their last hold-out in these depleted isles. Some of these species are particularly scarce and elusive, thinly distributed across the wide ranges of the forest, and so not at all easy to find, but it does mean that you never know quite what you are going to come across next, that there is always the possibility of discovering the unexpected. If I was a different kind of person, I could contact experts and specialist groups of botanical or entomological enthusiasts, and get them to lead the way, make proper use of their hard-won wisdom. But that has never really been my approach. As a child I wasn't ever much of a joiner, and that has not changed, really. My natural inclination has always been to just wander out alone, and see what I see, and miss what I miss. The Annie Dillard school of nature writing: to go and write about whatever I come upon, rather than deciding in advance what I want to see, and what I want to write about, and devising plans to best make it happen. Because one of the greatest joys of the natural world is its unpredictability.

Winding across the heath is a mounded ditch, several miles long, known as Bishop's Dyke, which roughly encloses some five hundred acres of boggy ground known as the Bishop of Winchester's Purlieu. John Wise, who wrote perhaps the first major study of the forest in 1863 – *The New Forest: Its History and Its Scenery* – makes mention of this dyke. He said that local peasants related that the bishop had been allocated a grant of as much land as he could crawl around on his hands and knees in a day. I'm not sure that, even then,

John Wise didn't suspect that he was having his leg pulled. It does sound an awful lot like the kind of tall tale that locals enjoy telling gullible anthropologists. But it does summon a compelling image, of a bishop in mitre and vestments, grovelling in the dirt, driven ever onward by his insatiable greed.

I was brought up about twenty miles away near Portsmouth, so this was never quite my local patch; coming to the forest always felt like I was coming somewhere special. We never had family holidays, only day trips, and this was always my favourite place to visit. It felt exotic to me, or at least what passed for exotic from within the curtailed purview of my childhood, which saw me almost never even leaving the county in which I had been born. It was the wide-open spaces that made it for me, great expanses without a fence in sight; that enabled me to run free, to follow my whims and wander pathless. It felt very different from everywhere else I knew, less controlled, less domesticated. By the time I got to my teens I would come and camp here when I could, but as soon as I was old enough my most urgent goal was to leave home and live elsewhere. There was a whole world to explore.

My early years were spent living in a bungalow in the village of Cowplain, a few miles inland from Portsmouth, though the succession of villages along the main London Road out of town – the A3 – had already begun to bleed into one another to become a semi-rural suburb that formed a commuter belt for the city's workers. Cowplain was situated in another former royal hunting forest, the Forest of Bere, though all that remained were a few isolated copses and enclosures. We lived on a road called Latchmore Forest Grove, no doubt named after a long-gone grove in a long-gone forest.

I don't really remember all that much before the fire. Early memories are vague, evanescent things, slipping and shifting through time and space. It is perhaps not surprising that some of my earliest memories relate to wildlife. There was a neighbour who had a tawny owl, a rescue bird, living in an aviary in his garden, and I recall the excitement of being allowed to visit. And I recall going to the garden of another neighbour, after dark, with torches in hand. We shone them underneath the garden shed, and lots of little eyes glinted back at us. I was jealous; I wished that we had a shed sheltering hedgehogs.

I can't picture the layout of our home at all, not even the bedroom that I shared with my older brother. It is perhaps easier to recall incidents that happened just once than the day-to-day background. One-off events stand out from the usual run of things, and so are more likely to stick with you. Although I can barely recall the house itself, I can picture the garden a little. Even then I was more of an outdoor child. The garden seemed remarkably big for such a small bungalow; there was an apple tree where wood pigeons cooed, there were rhododendrons and hydrangeas, and a scratchy clump of pampas grass. But these are fragmentary images; I can picture myself seeing them but I cannot turn my head to left or right, cannot place them in their proper context. It is like picking things out through a fog.

The fire changed all that. From that day on, my memories are clearer, harder, and are located in space and time. They form a sequence, a narrative, a story. There are moments in life that are full of such high drama that they stay with you for ever; close your eyes and you can summon them instantly, in every last detail, as if they are screened on the insides of your eyelids. Yet studies show that even these intensely remembered flashbulb memories cannot be entirely trusted; they can mutate over time according to our point of view. Memories are not stored intact in our minds just waiting to be fetched out; we have to reconstruct them from their constituent parts, piece by piece, every time.

I was woken by my mother in the hours of darkness, wrapped in a blanket, and carried through a burning building. At the door, the neighbours were all gathering. Arms reached out, and voices called: Here, here. I was handed to someone, carried out into the road. Two fire engines were just pulling up, their blue lights strobing, so that all the people milling about in the dark seemed to move in jerks, their backlit shadows dancing. The air was filled with the acrid smell of smoke. I looked back at the house and saw the flames coming from the roof, flames as high as the house itself. They looked strangely beautiful. That, that was the moment I can summon up in an instant in seemingly perfect detail. It was the moment at which life as I had known it came to a sudden stop, and a new one began.

The house did not stand much of a chance. It was a flimsy prefabricated structure made of lath and plaster over corrugated iron. I don't know if it had been constructed during the great wave of prefabs that were built immediately after the Second World War to help accommodate the displaced, or if it dated from earlier times, but this was the end of days for that house and almost everything in it.

My brother and I were taken home by neighbours, and placed on their sofa. My mother was there too, shell-shocked. My father arrived later, after he had been restrained by the firemen to stop him going back into the burning building to rescue some of our possessions. His eyes were blazing. He clapped his hands together and said: It's exciting, isn't it? And then he started laughing, a great bellowing laugh – and he couldn't stop.

It was Remembrance Sunday. The service was being screened on the late-night news. Surely it must have been a black-and-white TV, but I can distinctly remember a shower of blood-red poppies floating across the screen. This was 1966, the year that England won the World Cup. I can recall that day too, not because I had any particular interest in football but because it clashed with my uncle's wedding. The men in their cheap suits were all in one room, shouting at a TV set, while the women in their posh frocks were all in another, nibbling on canapés. And I, well, I didn't know quite where I should be.

Remembrance Sunday, 1966. Number one in the charts was the Four Tops singing 'Reach Out (I'll be There)'. Three days later would be the first broadcast of *Cathy Come Home*, written by Jeremy Sandford and directed by Ken Loach, which provoked a huge public outcry about the plight of homeless families. It was watched that night by twelve million people, a quarter of the population, but not by us; our TV had melted. Less than a month before the fire, a colliery spoil heap in the Welsh valleys had collapsed onto the village of Aberfan, inundating the village's primary school and killing well over a hundred children. These were the times.

So here is the story behind my own small personal drama, such as it is, as it has been passed down to me. Late that evening, after the kids were in bed, my father had climbed into the loft to investigate the source of a mysterious buzzing sound that had hovered above us for a week now, apparently coming from his self-installed central heating system. While up there, he trod on a loose wire, and a spark flew into the polystyrene loft insulation. For the record, polystyrene is not a good insulating material; it is highly flammable, liquifying as it burns. My father stuck his head out of the loft hatch and called to my mother to fetch a bucket of water. When she got back with it, he said: Too late. Get the boys out.

We moved into an abandoned house nearby, in the same street. The older couple who had lived there had recently died, one after the other, in quick succession. We mostly lived in one room, almost empty of furnishings. We had a single paraffin heater, and my mother would cook over a camping stove. I remember the overpowering stink of paraffin. I remember the bare brick walls, the darkness, and most of all the bitter cold of a house that felt haunted by its losses. We had Christmas there, we even had a Christmas tree, but it was not a place of celebration. I can't recall if we had running water, but we certainly had no hot water, for Friday night was bath night, and we would all troop off to the home of the family who had rescued us on the night of the fire, to take turns in their tub.

It was a pivotal moment in the life of our family. Things would never be the same again. There are unexpected forks in the road that can lead into a new and wholly unexpected landscape. Sometimes it has felt that

I have been forged by fire, that so much of who I am today, and the choices I have made along the way, can be traced back to that moment. I have had little interest in possessions, for I know that they can be lost in an instant. I have seldom even begun to let myself feel at home, and have rather treated everywhere I lived as just a stopover, for I know that all it takes is a spark. I have not sought out security, for I know that security is an illusion; and I have sought out emotional and practical self-sufficiency, for I know that ultimately the only person you can rely on is yourself. For much of my younger life, I kept no more belongings than could fit in a single bag, so that, whenever it suited, I could just get up and walk away. An option I took more times than I care to think about.

But I wonder now if this can really be true. For, if I had chosen a very different life, a life of security and stability, settled and rooted, I could just as easily turn around and say, of course I have chosen this life, it is a natural reaction to the insecurity I experienced as a child. Perhaps we just are the way that we are. Worse things happen. Everyone has something in their life, some pivotal moment that they see as a turning point, a key event in the story of their lives. We create a narrative of who we are, and why we are. This, therefore that. Perhaps if it hadn't been the fire, it would have been something else, and I would be sitting here now, exactly the same person, looking at a quite different route that led me to the same destination.

I recall, a few years after the fire, having a sudden shock of recognition the first time I heard the radio playing Peggy Lee's version of the Leiber and Stoller song, 'Is That All There Is?' The first verse, spoken rather than sung, seemed to be a near-perfect rendition of my own life experience. That song itself is based on a short story, 'Disillusionment', by Thomas Mann. It depicts someone talking about the transformative moments of their life, both good and bad, and feeling disappointed that they remain, nonetheless, fundamentally unchanged and unmoved.

The elements are all there: the family home, childhood, fire, night-time, and also, I think, the sense of powerlessness in the face of the random events of life. History repeats itself, as story, as song, as memoir. Is that all there is?

Perhaps because the story I tell myself about who I am is so grounded in this dramatic moment, I have at various stages in my life tried to give an account of this episode; thirty years ago, twenty years ago, ten years ago. It is as though I cannot quite leave it alone; time and time again I have found myself once again picking over the ruins. Every time the facts remain the same, and the memories too, for the most part. What I have struggled with has always been the meaning of that day, its meaning to me, how it may have shaped me, that moment that seemed to turn my life into a before and after. But I like to think that I have found my peace now, and am prepared to live with creative ambiguity.

TWO

The Shadow and the Substance

February 2019

I return to the forest without a destination in mind, my only goal an aimless walk in the woods, to just follow my nose and see where it leads me. That unlikely winter sun of my previous visit, just a few days ago in late January, is gone now; the sky is grey and lowering, as if it is pregnant with rain, and the air is perfectly still, so still and quiet that it is almost buzzing with silence. Nothing stirs out on the heath; it seems bereft of life. Sometimes winter days can be like that, when nothing seems to be moving and it feels as if the whole world is in suspension, just waiting for spring. I follow pony trails into a dense thicket of gorse, or furze as it is more often called here. The bushes are about ten feet high, so it is like being in a miniature woodland. Their brilliant yellow flowers have a distinctive scent of coconut. At last, I see a bird, static in a hawthorn bush. I look again, and see another, and the more I look, the more I see. That one bare little hawthorn is somehow concealing a flock of around thirty linnets, with rosy breasts and mossy brown backs, and a little red dab above the bill. It makes me wonder how I am ever going to see anything once the leaves are out.

The linnet was very much a bird of my childhood. I used to seek out their nests in the blackthorn scrub that encircled our house on the hill, that was in a kind of edgeland, neither town nor country. This scrubland was riddled with fox trails, but also with human-made dens that always seemed to contain sodden copies of *Mayfair* and *Health & Efficiency*, and was a haven for the linnets. But linnets are not doing so well now; they have recently been added to the red list of birds that are in trouble. Since 1970 their population has declined by more than fifty per cent. A similar decline in numbers has also been observed in many of the other farmland birds that kept me company on my daily walks as a child; the corn buntings and yellowhammers and skylarks. Not that linnets are uncommon, yet. The red list is more a mark of concern over a dramatic population fall than a measure of absolute rarity. I note that the herring gull has also recently joined the list, which may seem incredible to people who, like me, live in a place where they nest on every roof, are a regular early-morning alarm call, and will fight you for a sandwich.

A bird can be rare but recovering in numbers. A good example might be the bittern, reliant on large reed beds to call home. In Britain, it was down to its last few pairs, but a huge conservation effort has been made to save it, to preserve its very specific habitat requirements and even to expand on them, by creating new expanses of reed beds in places such as disused gravel pits. Dedicated conservationists can be very good at such targeted interventions, where local action can make a huge difference. It is the generalists, with a wide distribution, that are harder to cater for, and this is why the still rare and specialised bittern has now been taken off the red list, while the herring gull and the linnet have been added. It may sometimes seem that there is a give and take, that one creature becomes commoner as another becomes rarer; the range of one may contract while the range of another expands. It seems that it is all part of a natural cycle, the flux of life on earth. But each species is unique, irreplaceable, and we cannot ignore the fact that the overall trend of life, from plants to invertebrates, to birds and mammals, is falling inexorably downhill. In Britain there are forty million fewer birds for me to look at now than there were when I was a child.

In 2018 a study was published in the Proceedings of the National Institute of Science, of a research project led by Professor Yinon M. Bar-On, entitled 'The Biomass Distribution on Earth'. The goal was to compare the biomass of different classes of life rather than numbers of individuals, because very small things can come in dizzyingly large numbers. It is thought that there are more individual bacteria on earth than there are stars in the entire universe, and yet together they are thought to constitute no more than fifteen per cent of life on earth. It takes an awful lot of bacteria to weigh up to an oak tree, for instance.

When it came to life forms more closely related to us, the study had some startling findings. There are thought to be close to ten thousand species of birds on earth, but more than seventy per cent of those alive today are chickens. At any one moment, there are around twenty-five billion of them worldwide. The vast majority will be killed for food by the time they are six weeks old, even though a backyard hen can live for up to eight years. Sixty per cent of mammals consist of the handful of species we have learned how to domesticate, and thirty-six per cent of the remainder are, well, us. Just four per cent of mammals on earth are wild animals.

Nature reserves can be important as a place of last resort for threatened wildlife, but it is not enough to just create little pockets of life, oases in a desolate wasteland rendered almost lifeless by pesticides and monocultures and pollution. It puts me in mind of Joni Mitchell's tree museum, a place in which the living world is reduced to a few small fragments, which we can visit as an occasional reminder of what we have lost. We need somehow to press the reset button, and completely rethink how we see our relationship with the earth. We need to reinvent ourselves as collaborators rather than conquerors. It makes me wonder if the New Forest, a living, working landscape that serves both man and nature, and has remained substantially unchanged for a thousand years or more, could offer us a kind of model of a better way to manage our environment.

The New Forest dates from the time of the Norman conquest as a recognisable entity. This was not just an occupation; it was a conquest, absolute – and, following their victory at the Battle of Hastings, the Normans could do pretty much whatever they liked. And what they mostly seemed to like was hunting. They established deer parks and deer forests all over the country, the New Forest being the very first of these, close to their newly established capital in Winchester. They imported their favoured species of deer, the fallow, from the Mediterranean, and it still remains the most numerous of the forest's several types of deer.

I enter the woods, following the path of a stream rather than a track. A trail of long-tailed tits is strung between the trees, bouncing one by one from treetop to treetop. The little birds twirl at the tips of the most slender twigs, in constant motion, like a troupe of tiny acrobats. Soon these winter parties will be breaking up and the birds will begin pairing off to start building their elaborate nests. Then I notice an unexpected movement in an old oak just ahead of me, like a branch coming to life. I can scarcely believe that I had been unable to see it until it made a move. It is the size of a buzzard, but while buzzards are shaggy and baggy in a way that is somehow endearing, this bird could never be described as such; it is sleek and fierce; it is a goshawk.

She launches herself suddenly from her perch and away from me. She does not drop down beneath the canopy, but flies at great speed right through it, twisting and turning between the branches with a seemingly impossible precision. I assume that the moment is over, but she stops and perches in another oak just a further thirty yards or so away from me. This never happens. I have watched a lot of goshawks and have almost never seen one perched. The bird is a ghost; it flashes past the corner of your eye and is gone, vanished in an instant, leaving you to think: Wait, what? You don't surprise a goshawk; a goshawk surprises you. I may walk in silence, always aiming towards invisibility, but this is a bird whose eyesight is ten times as acute as mine. Seeing one feels like an honour; it feels that if she did not want me to see her, then I would not have seen her.

The bird has her back to me, but her head is turned so that she can glare at me with her intent orange eye. I watch the goshawk, and the goshawk watches me. We both seem transfixed, and the moment seems to last an impossibly long time. It is as if the bird is defiant. Why should I move? It's my wood; you move. Finally, without warning, she springs a second time. But it is still not the end, for she stops again, just one more tree further away. It feels as though she is leading me on, to an unknown destination in the darkest depths of the woods. Come, come. Follow, follow. Deeper, deeper.

Wandering onwards, I reach the ruins of an old wood. It is large enough that I can barely see to its outer limits. Every tree is dead, though most are still standing. They have all lost their bark, leaving their trunks as white as bone, and their remaining branches reach for the sky like antlers. The ground beneath the skeleton trees is piled deep with shed bark and a brash of fallen twigs, so that almost nothing can grow. The place looks like a vision of the future, post-apocalyptic. And after the devastation caused by Dutch elm disease, we are now faced with ash dieback, acute oak decline and chronic oak dieback. It is not a good time to be a tree. Sometimes it seems as if it is not a good time to be a human either; it is hard not to feel overwhelmed by anxiety for the future, a kind of existential helplessness in the face of overwhelming environmental degradation, and the feeling that there is nothing we can do that would make a difference. This environmental dread is hardly a pathology, but rather a rational response to the way the world is turning; to remain unconcerned about the future of the earth and the path that we are taking now requires an act of wilful blindness. But it is not an entirely new experience. It is there, vividly, in so many of the poems written by John Clare in the early 1800s, in which he grieves, achingly, for the loss of the commons of his childhood and their thriving natural life, devastated by the Enclosure Acts. It would perhaps be reductive to assume that it was this grief that led to him spending the last decades of his life confined to an asylum, but it cannot have helped:

> Unbounded freedom ruled the wandering scene
> Nor fence of ownership crept in between
> To hide the prospect of the following eye
> Its only bondage was the circling sky . . .
> . . . Now this sweet vision of my boyish hours
> Free as spring clouds and wild as summer flowers
> Is faded all – a hope that blossomed free,
> And hath been once, no more shall ever be.

Inclosure came, and trampled on the grave
Of labour's rights and left the poor a slave
And memory's pride ere want to wealth did bow
Is both the shadow and the substance now.

From 'The Mores'

THREE

The Tragedy of the Commons

February 2019

I pass into a plantation of Douglas fir, and the blue and great tits that abound in the oak woods are immediately replaced by a handful of the little coal tits that prefer conifers. For the past century or so, the Crown lands of the forest have been managed by the Forestry Commission, so there is some commercial woodland here, though the understanding has been that these plantations are not allowed to account for more than a relatively small acreage of the forest. And as public awareness has grown with the understanding that all woods are not equal, and that large, evenly-spaced stands comprised of only fast-growing conifers may result in something close to an environmental wasteland, some have been replaced after felling by a mixed woodland more in keeping with the spirit of the place. It is a matter of balance, of course, a balance that has not always been kept. Back in the sixties, it looked for a time as though the delicate stasis of the forest was in real jeopardy; the Forestry Commission was busy draining the mires and cutting down ancient woodlands to replace them with conifers, and it was perhaps only the dedicated work of conservationists such as Colin Tubbs that got them to wind their neck in. Grumbling about the choices made by the commission still seems to be something of a local sport, and it was probably ever thus; W. H. Hudson was writing about local dissatisfaction with the management of the Crown lands a hundred and twenty years ago, and I have no doubt that, a millennium ago, residents would have had a few choice words about Norman deer-forestry practices.

The wood I am standing in is made up of towering, full-grown trees, rather than being a working plantation, and walking in the scented half-light between these vast monumental columns on a soft bed of fallen needles in an almost cathedral silence makes it imposing in its own way. It is almost as if the lifelessness is part of the appeal.

At least the oaks are no longer being harvested for

shipbuilding, as they were in the eighteenth century. Cut down an ancient oak and you are not just taking one life. Hundreds of species – of fungi and lichens, of invertebrates and more – are wholly dependent on the oak, more, perhaps, than on any other tree species. Destroy an oakwood and you are destroying an entire ecosystem. Cut down an oak tree and it is not enough to plant an acorn in its place. A full-grown oak may bear more than a quarter of a million leaves, while a new sapling has four or five. It will conceivably take centuries to replace what has been lost. Planting oaks for timber was in some ways an incredible act of faith, or perhaps of hubris, that there is continuity, that there is a future reaching out far beyond us. Plant an oak and it will not be ready to crop in your lifetime, in your children's lifetime, in your grandchildren's lifetime. The oaks planted in Ravens Nest Inclosure had barely got going when the age of the wooden ship came to an end. And still they grow, more than two centuries later.

Far off between the tree trunks I can see something incongruously white and square; a hut or a shed perhaps. As I slowly approach it begins to resolve itself into something more recognisable. Could it really be? An ice-cream van, in the middle of the woods, in the middle of winter. We're not in Kansas any more.

It seems implausible, but becomes more explicable when I realise that I have stumbled upon a car park in the woods. Here is the Rhinefield ornamental drive, and the tall trees circular trail. The early Victorians planted the area with redwoods and Douglas firs that now, at two hundred years old, are the biggest and tallest trees in the forest, though still babies compared to their Californian cousins. And there is an arboretum here too – the Blackwater arboretum, one of two in the forest. An actual tree museum. It is the complete opposite of what I was expecting when I set off into the heart of the woods. Out of curiosity, I head through the gates. In a large clearing amidst the giant conifers is a well-kept grassy area where the widely spaced trees all have plaques to tell you what they are. Volunteers with hi-vis yellow vests are pushing wheelbarrows around the trails. There are comfortable benches and attractive wooden sculptures of giant acorns and oak leaves. It is all very civilised, the kind of place you might hope to end up in after death, if you were lucky.

I attempt to retrace my steps through the woods,

thinking I might go back to where I saw the goshawk, and get hopelessly lost. Fine with me. Lost is good. Eventually I come upon a well-worn trail, and a family with mountain bikes stop and pore over my map to give me directions. I am impressed by how far I am from where I thought I was. I have wandered miles off-track. Just as I cross a wooden bridge over a stream at the edge of the woods and onto the open heath, the skies open.

The black, laden clouds that have been hovering menacingly all day seem to drop from the sky until they almost touch the ground. The light suddenly fades and the rain is torrential. Out on the lawn where there is no shelter taller than a gorse bush, the ponies look dejected; their heads hung low to the ground, their manes streaming. Any dog-walkers must have run for cover, but I am happy to stride out into the centre of the storm. Wild weather makes the place seem just that little bit wilder, makes me feel that, much as we try to domesticate the world, it will still always retain an element that is untameable. I feel like raging at the world, like King Lear on his blasted heath. The ground begins to flood astonishingly quickly, and soon I find myself having to skip from one grassy hummock to the next across instant rivulets, as if from island to island. And then, as quickly as it had begun, the storm is over. The skies clear and the late-afternoon sun streams in slantwise, the first sunshine I have seen all day. And there are rainbows.

Those sodden ponies on the heath may be free-roaming, but they are not truly wild. Each one is tagged and owned and licensed, in part to keep the breed pure. Stallions are put out only for about two weeks each spring, to cover the mares. The ponies are rounded up from late summer onwards in what are known as drifts, and surplus foals are sold off on sale days, held several times each autumn and winter in the sale yards at Beaulieu Road. Ownership is in the hands of around seven hundred commoners, whose right of pasture resides with the property rather than the individual. They need to have enough land to accommodate their stock when they are off the forest. There is not a great deal of money to be made out of commoning, and property prices in the area have escalated dramatically. Newly wealthy property owners may not want to retain their commoners' rights, so the vast majority of the commoners have obtained their rights through inheritance.

Rights of pasture extend to cattle as well as horses, and there are almost as many of each roaming the forest. Cattle are just not so obvious, as they tend to stay in their herds while the ponies scatter themselves more widely. There are a few donkeys in the forest too, and you will sometimes see a little Shetland pony trailing along behind the New Forest ponies with that slightly confused look that they always seem to have. Rounding up all the animals is a challenge, and involves a good deal of teamwork and coordination, but the animals tend to be hefted to a particular stretch of the forest, and the ponies may even have their own favoured shades where they go to shelter each day. It is not all as random as it may look at first sight.

As well as these rights of pasture, there are rights of pannage, which allow for pigs to be put out for a few weeks each autumn, to take advantage of the year's fall of acorns and beech mast. The pigs thrive on acorns, while they are poisonous to cattle and horses, so everybody wins. There is also the right of estovers – entitling the commoners to collect a limited amount of firewood. And there were once other rights, which are now no longer in use: the rights of turbary and marl – to dig for peat and lime. These ancient rights of common are closely guarded, and even adjudicated upon in case of dispute, through the Verderer's Court in Lyndhurst, and have been for centuries. The verderers are responsible for administering forest law, while also appointing a team of employees known as agisters, who assist in the management of the commoners' livestock.

This is a relict landscape, which has endured almost unchanged for centuries, against all odds, while the world around it has been carved up. There was a time when a vast proportion of the British countryside would have looked much like it. Over the course of three centuries there were a succession of Enclosure Acts – more than five thousand of them – in which landowners took away these rights, fenced off the common lands and turned them into monocultures, largely creating the rural landscape we see today, in pursuit of greater profits. Similarly, in the Highlands, the crofters were ejected from their crofts to make way for large-scale sheep farming. All those Enclosure Acts combined took away the rural population's traditional rights over ten thousand square miles of land, a third of the land area of England. The landless peasantry, completely dependent on being able to put their few animals out to graze, or to collect fuel for their fires, were left completely dispossessed. A subsistence economy turned to a wage economy. Most people who had no land of their own to fall back on ended up going to the towns, where, just as the Industrial Revolution began to kick in, they would become a pool of available labour. The New Forest was saved from this fate largely by virtue of the soil being unsuited for conventional agriculture.

The Friends of the Earth campaigner Guy Shrubsole is author of the book *Who Owns England?* It was a challenging piece of research, for land ownership in this country is alarmingly opaque, seemingly hidden behind layer upon layer of legal veils. One of the answers he found to his titular question is that a shocking thirty per cent of it is still owned by the aristocracy – the aristocracy being, as the late Duke of Westminster notoriously put it, people who made sure to have an ancestor who was a close personal friend of William the Conqueror. More than the same again, another thirty per cent, is owned by new money, ranging from old-new money – families who made their fortunes in the Industrial Revolution, or perhaps the slave trade – to new-new money – hedge-fund managers and oligarchs. This is the situation across the UK as a whole – sixty per cent of the land is owned by a third of one per cent of the population. Most of the remainder is owned by the Church, the army, or corporations such as the water boards, or even by offshore corporations. There is, therefore, not much left over for everyone else. This is why property prices are so unfeasibly high; because the vast majority of people in Britain – 99.66 per cent of us – have been left to fight over scraps. Just five per cent of the land area of Britain is available for us to live on. If we can afford it.

First they take the land, then they draw up deeds of title to establish legal ownership, then they build fences to keep us out, then they try to make sure we don't even know who they are. A huge amount of effort has been put into concealing just how unequal our society really is. Ever get the feeling you've been cheated?

> The law locks up the man or woman
> Who steals the goose from off the common
> But lets the greater villain loose
> Who steals the common from the goose

The law demands that we atone
When we take things we do not own
Yet leaves the lords and ladies fine
Who take things that are yours and mine

The poor and wretched don't escape
If they conspire the law to break
This must be so but they endure
Those who conspire to make the law

The law locks up the man or woman
Who steals the goose from off the common
And geese will still a common lack
Until they go and steal it back

Traditional *c.* 1800

FOUR

Newroz

March 2019

The seasons don't really have a clear-cut beginning and end. They bleed into one another seamlessly, as the world turns its relentless path around the sun. This is why we create our own markers, tell ourselves that when the daffodils bloom, or the first cuckoo calls, then spring is definitely here. My own personal cypher, from my years in the hills of Wales during the nineties, depicted in my book *Deep Country*, has always been the arrival of the curlews from the coast. It would always be the second week of March, and I would wait for them impatiently; when I heard my first calling curlew of the year, I would tell myself that spring was finally here, even though I knew perfectly well that there would still be more snow to come, later in March or even in April.

Accordingly, I came for a brief visit to the forest in the second week of March, in the hope of seeing a displaying curlew, and found one solitary bird. This is probably the last place in lowland Britain where I still had much of a chance, for the curlew is in deep, deep trouble, and in rapid decline. In recent years its numbers have crashed catastrophically, with very poor rates of breeding success, largely due to changes in land use and no doubt also due to climate change. Its range has contracted into the upland moors of northern Britain, with a few holdouts here in the New Forest. Their gradual disappearance is not just a local concern, for the British population of curlews forms a significant share of the entire world's population. If we can't save them here, then we perhaps cannot save them at all. I find it hard to bear the thought of a world without that endlessly evocative bubbling trill over the winter marshes or the heaths and moors of summer. There would be no more spring.

I have returned to the forest on a beautiful sunny day for the spring equinox, which I suppose is as good a marker as any. Solstices and equinoxes at least form a logically consistent way to divide up the year's cycle.

The blackthorns, which flower before their leaves begin to bud, are a froth of white. The willows are furry with catkins, and the hazel catkins too are blooming. There are celandines beneath the hedgerows, and the first of the violets, the early dog violet. I begin my walk in a large enclosure of mostly deciduous woodland, fenced off to keep out the grazing animals. It is a very different environment from the open wood pasture. There are dense shrubs beneath the trees, and a rich green ground layer, even though the foresters have been busy so there are not the ancient trees and deadwood that are found elsewhere. But I suppose that the mix is a good thing; it helps diversify the environment to benefit a wider range of living things.

As I walk the empty rides, I see my first butterflies of the year. Most are bright lemon-yellow brimstones, but there is a single red admiral. Most red admirals migrate here, and arrive much later, but a handful manage to overwinter, and get themselves a head start. At first it seems that I have the woods entirely to myself, but then I hear a muttering in the distance, a multitude of voices. At a crossing in the woods is a school party of perhaps fifty boys, with their gowned and bearded teachers. They are not dressed for the country, but in crisp black-and-white uniforms, and most are wearing kippahs. A day trip for a class of Jewish schoolboys, I suppose. I am used to walking in remote places where, if I see anyone at all, it is likely to be a hardened hill-walker, and am having to get used to the idea that things are different here, that my walks will be filled with unexpected encounters.

If there is a point to public land, it is that it is open to everyone. And yet visiting can still feel, for much of the time, a markedly monocultural experience. It is a complicated truth that the fourteen per cent or so of our population that come from minority communities make up only one per cent of visitors to our national parks. It is not down to a lack of interest, I am sure, but more a lack of opportunity. Some of this is due to economic factors; people with fewer resources are likely to live further from areas of natural beauty, are less likely to have access to transport, and also less likely to have access to free time. This, of course, may be true of the urban poor more generally. But I think a main driver of this may be more a sense of exclusion, not solely a matter of either choice or opportunity, and can affect even those who are not constrained by resources. In a country where land ownership is already completely sewn up, in ways that are not always transparent, and wealth and the access to land that it brings are largely handed down through the generations, people may feel that they can never easily belong, and may quite reasonably wonder whether they will ever be made to feel welcome in places where no one looks like them, in what has the appearance of white space. At least the New Forest, relatively close to large urban centres and relatively easy to access even by public transport, may be a little less exclusive than most.

Let me tell you a spring tale from my past; one that I always tend to recall at this time of year. When I was living in my cottage in the mountains of Wales, I had a visit from a group of Kurdish and Moroccan friends, who drove all the way from London to see me. They had come to celebrate Newroz, Kurdish New Year, which coincides with the spring equinox. While the others came in to warm themselves by the fire, my Kurdish friend Saadulla stayed outside, gazing at the view, and I went to join him. As we looked over the wide green valley below, and the line of mountains, still capped with snow, that ringed the horizon, he said to me: I had no idea there were places like this here. He looked over at me, with a misty-eyed look: It reminds me so much of home, he said. He had come as a refugee fifteen years earlier, and had never been back. All those years he had lived and worked in the city, and had little opportunity to escape it. When he had to leave Wales after a few days' stay, he left a pair of shoes under the stairs to mark a promise that he would return. But he never did, stopped by ill-health. I looked out at that view every morning; it was a view that I never grew tired of. I knew just what vegetables I could grow at that altitude and in that poor soil. I knew which glades to visit, and when, if I wanted to forage for wild mushrooms or berries. I knew the territories of all the local birds and where they nested. I knew every inch of every wood within daily walking distance. There is a huge value in this kind of localism, of embedding yourself so deeply in your local environment. But there is also a value in the perspective of an outsider – that first impression, that visceral emotional response. We need to recognise that other eyes will see things that we could never see. We need to consider that the whole world belongs to everyone, not just to those who have staked their claim most forcefully.

I pass through a gate and step out from under the trees, beginning a gentle climb onto the wide-open heath. A solitary hawthorn holds a single portly cock bullfinch, glorious with his neat black cap and his rosy breast, nipping at the new buds. I am sure they are delicious; as a kid I used to snack on newly sprouted hawthorn leaves myself. Everywhere there are stone-chats; I have never seen so many. Mostly they are paired up, and seem to be on every bush, flitting from one furze top to another, and calling, calling. The males in particular are very attractive birds, with their jet-black heads, white collars and bright orange breasts. Their relentless chinking calls do sound rather like the sound of two stones being tapped together. I have not heard the term used elsewhere, but W. H. Hudson, writing about the forest in 1903, refers to them as fuzz-jacks, which strikes me as a charming name for them, and one that I have at this very moment decided that I shall adopt. Hudson is perhaps best known for his writings on the Argentinian pampas where he grew up, and he may be better remembered there than here, but after coming to England in his thirties he wrote a series of books on rural life and on nature set mainly in the south of England. The best-known of these is *A Shepherd's Life*, but his book *Hampshire Days* is set for its first half in the New Forest, before he drifts off to other parts of the county, notably to the vicinity of Selborne, the home village of Gilbert White. I shall perhaps return to him, for he paints a fine picture of the life of the forest well over a century ago, at around the time my grandfather was born hereabouts – although the book does include a rather unfortunate chapter in which he attempts to divide the Hampshire peasantry into four distinct types, by colouring and body shape, by intellectual capacity and moral character. Perhaps inevitably, he concludes that by far the rarest and most admirable of his categories just happens to contain those people who are most like him. I wonder where he would have placed me within this taxonomy.

On a dull day, the buzzards will settle in the trees, hunched up as if in a bad mood, and you will only see them if you happen to pass by and flush them, but on a glorious sunny day like today, they will rise. With the wide views afforded me from high on the heath, I can see two or three circling at any moment, sometimes above me, sometimes below. And then, as I approach the summit of a gentle hillside, a small bird flies up and circles directly above me, beginning to sing. A lark ascending. It is not a skylark, though, but a woodlark, short-tailed and round-winged, and rather than the skylark's joyful torrent, its song is gentler, more melodious, filled with more complicated emotions. Its generic name in Latin gives you the idea – *Lullula* – and its name in French – *lulu*. It is perhaps not much of a looker but its song is highly regarded among the few who have the good luck to hear it; there are some who claim it to have the most beautiful, emotive song of any of our songbirds. Much rarer than the familiar skylark, the woodlark is a specialist of lowland heath rather than grassland. The New Forest is very much its heartland, and, indeed, a little further along the trail I see two more, a pair together. I have been looking out for them, but had not seen them on my earlier visits. While a few overwinter, many head off to the Continent, to return in the spring, and they are not the most visible of birds, at least until they begin their song flights.

It is a curious thing that the birds with the most appealing songs tend to be dull in colour – the larks, the nightingales, the thrushes, some of the warblers; none of them are much to look at, while the showy, brilliantly coloured birds very often seem to have a call that sounds like nails on a blackboard. It is as if there is a rule that says they can have one good thing but not the other; if they can't attract a mate with their looks, then at least they have that voice. I wonder if the same rule applies to writers; I wonder if I was significantly uglier then I might just be a better writer. I also wonder if I would make the trade.

I put in my hearing aids to extend my range, lie down in a grassy patch among the heather, and close my eyes to give the bird its due. To be honest, I cannot capture it in its full glory; I pick up just a few scattered notes. But deafness is good for the imagination; you become adept at having conversations in which all you hear are a few key words, and you fill in the gaps with intuition and whatever clues you can shepherd together. I believe that, in part, I owe my attentiveness to my deafness.

Lying in the long grass in the sunshine, watching clouds, surrounded by the buzz of insects and the song of birds. It is a picture of childhood, and not just for me. I am reminded of John Clare's last poem, 'I Am!' We leave him sleeping as he did when he was a child, and this is his final expression of self, how he chooses to represent his identity – as the boy on the common:

> I long for scenes where man hath never trod
> A place where woman never smiled or wept
> There to abide with my creator, God,
> And sleep as I in childhood sweetly slept,
> Untroubling and untroubled where I lie
> The grass below – above the vaulted sky.

I am distracted from the trail I am on by a distinctive mound among the heather: an ancient barrow. It is perhaps fifteen or twenty feet high and about thirty feet long. It has a gentle dip at its summit, like that of a long-extinct volcano, and what looks like the vestiges of a ditch all around it, although that may have been caused by ponies walking in circles. Its banks have been mined by rabbits; perhaps they like the elevation, to give them a better view of any approaching threats. As I climb the mound, I notice something in the spoils outside a rabbit burrow. It looks like a knapped flint. And then I see another, and another. Points and scrapers.

These barrows dotted across the forest are Bronze Age in origin, but perhaps this one had been built on an older Mesolithic or Neolithic site. It might be that it is an illusion, that natural processes have chipped these stones in a way that makes them look like tools. Or maybe it is the rabbits honing their skills, getting ready for the revolution.

At the time of the last glacial maximum, the entirety of what is now Scotland, Wales and Ireland was subsumed by a massive ice sheet a kilometre or more deep, and most of England too. Only a strip of southern England, still connected to the Continent, remained ice-free. Here would have been a land resembling the arctic tundra, grazed over by herds of woolly mammoth and woolly rhinoceros, hunted by cave lions and cave bears and cave hyenas. If it sounds like caves must have been prime real estate back then, we should allow for a degree of cognitive bias. We might think that because the remains of these beasts are only found in caves, then therefore they must have all lived in caves. But, of course, if they had ended their days out in the open, exposed to the elements, then their remains would not have endured. I am sure that many of these beasts lived and died without ever once setting foot inside a cave. Because they lived in places where there were no caves. Such as here, for instance.

As the ice began to retreat, trees and scrub began to invade, first the early pioneer species, such as birch and pine. There would then have been a natural succession leading up to the climax vegetation, which here would have been predominantly oakwood. The forest would have been grazed by the tarpan, the wild ancestor of the domestic horse; by the aurochs, the ancestor of cattle; by wild boar; and by a range of deer species. The numbers of these would have been controlled through predation, by wolves and bears and lynxes. Now the forest is grazed by our ponies, cattle, and the pigs that are put out in autumn for pannage, to harvest the fallen acorns, as well as by deer both wild and introduced. We farm the horses, cattle and pigs, and we cull the deer. We are the wolves. And while the world might be a better place if we did not domesticate and eat so many animals, these beasts have their natural place in the landscape. Almost by accident, we have seemingly recreated the conditions of the primeval forest. Even the larger ponds here, which have been made by humans flooding disused marl and gravel pits, and are home to some of the forest's most distinctive animal and plant life, are perhaps a simulacrum of the ponds that would once have been created in the forest by the work of beavers. This is a land that has been occupied for millennia, but that has been manipulated and worked in a way that has benefited both people and nature, and has left it a great reservoir of biodiversity.

The presumption has been that the patchwork landscape here arose when early human settlers, the Neolithic and Bronze Age farmers, cleared areas of woodland for agriculture, but the soil was so poor that it was soon spent, and no longer suitable for anything other than rough grazing. And those grazing animals then put a stop to woodland regeneration taking place. But the evidence points to a slightly more complicated picture. Analysis of ancient pollen samples from peat cores suggests that, while some of the heathland may well have been cleared and cultivated in the distant past, there are also heaths and mires that have never supported woodland since the time this was all tundra. And there is a logical problem to be answered too; if the heaths of the forest are filled with species, from flowers to invertebrates to reptiles, whose life cycles are wholly dependent on a heathland environment, how would all these species have ever arisen if there was no native heathland in the first place? As I stand at the summit of the burial mound, king of the castle, I look out on a view that might perhaps have remained virtually unchanged for millennia. The person buried beneath this hillock must have seen what I see, but thought about it in ways that I cannot even begin to imagine.

FIVE

The White Hart

March–April 2019

Every time I take the train to the New Forest, I have to pass by my home town. The train doesn't go all the way into Portsmouth, but does stop off at Cosham, which was my local station as I was growing up. From the moment it pulls into the station, I feel a strange sense of being on edge, as if I can't wait for the train to get going again. This sense of unease, I am sure, has very little to do with Portsmouth, and a lot to do with me. I think it must be down to the fact that I spent my last years there itching to be old enough to get going, and to see the wider world. For me, Portsmouth became characterised as that place that you want to leave.

It was almost a year after the fire before we were able to settle somewhere else. I presume it took that long for the insurance to be sorted, and the land to be disposed of. My hope had been that we would find ourselves somewhere more rural, but I was too young to have an opinion that counted. For a while it looked as though we might end up moving into a houseboat, my father's latest obsession. My father was a man of great enthusiasms, which would suddenly wither and die as quickly as they had appeared, only to be replaced by the next one. He had got as far as finding a suitable boat, but was ultimately unable to find a mooring for it. I am sure my mother breathed a sigh of relief. Too cramped, she thought, too dangerous, plus we would have all been in each other's hair. But she didn't really get to have a say in such matters either. We finally ended up moving much closer to town. Overlooking the city is a long, low ridge of chalk downland called Portsdown Hill, an outlier of the South Downs. It is capped by a series of huge brick forts known as Palmerston's Follies. Portsmouth is surrounded by defensive forts built by the Victorians to defend against an anticipated French attack that never happened. Those on the hill were ridiculed as follies because they faced inland, away from the sea, though they were actually intended as a defence against a land-based attack, so would perhaps not have been as useless as they looked, had the fears of alien invasion not been so overblown. This ridge is also studded by a chain of old chalk quarries, which makes it look as if the hill has had chunks bitten out of it by a dragon. Our home was in one of these abandoned quarries – there was an eighty-foot chalk cliff right behind the house, overgrown with ivy. Yes, I had basically become Stig of the Dump. The quarry also contained a couple of derelict cottages, flint-faced but with chalk walls. There is a reason why chalk is not widely used as a building material, and these empty cottages were crumbling and damp, but they were at least a great playground when I was a kid, and later a useful hide from which to watch the garden foxes that denned behind them. There was a fine expansive view south from our new home, over Langstone and Portsmouth harbours, with the island of Portsea between them, and across the Solent to the Isle of Wight beyond.

Portsmouth was atypical for a Southern town, and in some ways was more like the industrial cities of the North, being hugely dependent on a single heavy industry; that being shipbuilding at the naval dockyard. The docks were overwhelmingly the largest employer in town, and most other businesses were in some way dependent on them. My own father apprenticed there from the age of fourteen, joining his father, who worked there too, after a career in the Merchant Navy. But by the time I was growing up, the industry was already in steep decline and they were laying off thousands of men every year. Portsmouth was beginning to feel like a place without a purpose. This was not helped by the heavy shadow of war hanging over it; even decades after Armistice there were bomb sites everywhere you looked. Every row of terraced housing seemed to have a boarded-up gap, filled with rubble and buddleia and willowherb, the neighbouring houses propped up with oak beams.

My father set up an engineering business from home, focused on garden machinery; mostly he repaired and sold parts for chainsaws. When he was not working, he was tinkering with cars. He would buy crashed cars, chop them up and recombine them into his own creations. Our driveway was always filled with scrap. While my father could turn his hand to anything practical, my brother and I were never encouraged to take an interest; rather we were told before we even started school that we would be the first in the family to go to university. Our destiny was to get an education; both of my parents, growing up during wartime, had been forced to leave school early and without qualifications in order to help support their families, and felt keenly that their horizons had been limited by the lack of an education. My mother would go on to take an Open University degree later in life, as if to prove to herself that she had been held back only by want of the right opportunity. And they were undoubtedly right that a good education can give you more choices in life; although many of those choices might not have been ones they would have foreseen. They most likely thought of education as a route to stability, through gaining professional qualifications in something steady; such as medicine, or law, or accountancy. While I was more inclined to think of it as a route to freedom.

All around the quarry where we lived was open grassland, dotted with patches of scrub, of hawthorn and blackthorn; public land, common land. In places it was kept mown short by the council, for recreational purposes, for strollers and dog-walkers, but in other areas it was left untouched, and grew as wild-flower meadow. In spring it would be thick with butterflies and bees and grasshoppers. And the flowers of chalk grassland; bird's-foot-trefoil and horseshoe vetch, red campion and ragged robin, lady's bedstraw and rest harrow, eyebright and wild thyme. In late spring the orchids would come: great colonies of common spotted orchids and pyramidal orchids, and sometimes a lucky find like a bee orchid, an exquisite gem. Later in the year would come the autumn lady's-tresses orchids, elegant white spirals that even grew on our garden lawn. It was a great place for a kid to run wild, especially one given to solitary pursuits. For a deaf child, conversation was too much like hard work; being on my own was like a holiday.

The overgrown quarry in which we lived proved to be remarkable too. Facing south out to sea, it might be the very first patch of greenery that newly arrived migrant birds would come to. I would wait for them impatiently each spring, and one day I would wake to a huge fall of migrant warblers; willow warblers by the dozens, blackcaps and garden warblers and lesser whitethroats. There would be birds that didn't nest locally, such as redstarts and pied flycatchers, birds that, with luck, might decide to stay, such as spotted flycatchers, and occasionally something extraordinary, such as a wryneck contorting itself on our lawn. The whole process would be repeated in reverse each autumn, though it would be a little more staggered, as the birds stopped to feed at the last-chance saloon before setting off into the unknown.

The path I am following down off the heath and back towards the woods leads me through a car park hidden among the gorse. There seems to be a fuzz-jack perched on the topmost spray of every bush, but there are no cars, and in fact, despite the wide views and the glorious weather, I have not seen a single person for the two hours or so I have been out on the heath. A sign announces that the car park will be closed for five months, for the breeding season, and directs drivers to alternative areas. It does not affect me as I choose to travel either by using public transport or on foot, but irrespective of that, it does seem reasonable that the rights of public access need to be kept in balance with the land's value to nature. A further sign says that this has been identified as a key area for nesting waders. These would be curlews, lapwings, redshanks and snipe, all of which are in trouble, and all of which are ground

nesters and therefore extremely vulnerable to disturb-
ance, perhaps especially by walkers with dogs off the
leash. They are all highly strung birds, inclined to fly
into a screaming panic at the first hint of an approach.
The advice urges visitors to stick to the main trails, and
though my own inclination has always been to go
off-trail as much as possible, and to follow the path of
most resistance, I am happy to abide, for while I would
like to see these birds, I would like even more for them
to survive.

By the forest edge is a large pool, surrounded by a
short sward being grazed by ponies. At their feet on the
lawn stands a solitary lapwing, close to the water. I
deliberately keep my distance, so as not to disturb it.
These are underrated birds, I always think, and their
decline is a great loss. They have such an evocative call,
and a striking display flight. A winter flock of them
passing overhead with their big butterfly wings is always
a sight to behold. Their backs are a beautiful metallic
green like no other bird, and they have a long, graceful
crest that blows in the breeze.

Across a clearing in the woods, staying just within
cover, is a herd of fallow deer, nineteen of them by my

count, which takes a while, as they are in constant motion. They are all does; a single-sex herd. They range widely at night, but in the day-time they tend to be shyer and remain within the cover of the remoter thickets. This is only the second herd I have seen in my visits so far this year, but this is largely a matter of the season. In the winter the night is long enough, but as summer comes, and the hours of darkness shorten, they will be forced to spend more time grazing during daylight. Most of this herd have the traditional white dapples on chestnut, some are darker, and just one is pure white. Not an albino but a colour variant, not all that rare but still a striking sight, and one that seems to have impressed many before, to the point of embedding itself in the culture; there are an awful lot of pubs called the White Hart.

I remember the very first time I camped out in the New Forest. It was with my school's wildlife club, and it was the very last year that wild camping was still allowed in the forest; after that it would be designated camp-sites only. Early in the morning I emerged from my tent. The lapwings that nested nearby were displaying overhead – they were more common then – and a trail of deer was crossing the heath and returning to the woods, led by a splendid white buck with a fine head of antlers.

As I am watching the deer, I am approached by an older couple, the first people I have seen in hours. I point out the deer to them, which they hadn't noticed, but the solitary white deer has disappeared into the undergrowth. We talk about what a fine spring day it is, and the man comments on the butterflies, but says it doesn't really feel like spring until the migrant birds are here. He hasn't seen any yet; he would have expected the very first by now, to have at least heard his first chiffchaff. But he supposed that it depended on things like wind direction, and that in a couple of weeks' time they would all come flooding in, and the woods would come alive again. I'll be back for that, I said.

And I am, standing on a little wooden footbridge looking down at the sluggish waters of the Beaulieu River. Further downstream towards the sea, it is tidal and looks like a proper river; here in its upper reaches it is no more than a stream, winding lazily through the woods, narrow enough that in places a fallen tree is enough to make a natural crossing. Overhanging the banks beside the bridge are blackthorns in peak bloom, so dense with pure white blossom that they look overwhelmed by a sudden snowfall. Just in view are a pair of mandarin ducks that are watching me cautiously, waiting for me to make a move. The female is a pretty, understated little duck in dappled grey and with an eye-ring and eye-stripe like Tutankhamun's mask, but the drake is something else altogether. Beneath his red bill he has a lion's mane of feathers; he has a crest of metallic blue and green and purple, he has black and white bars and patches of copper and bronze, and he has two elegant sails above his back that seem to have no possible function. This is a bird of startling exoticism. They are native to China and Japan, but since their escape from wildfowl collections in the 1930s they have gradually spread across the country, until now there are probably more of them here than there are in any of their native lands. These are forest ducks, that can fly at great speed through dense woodland, and which rely on tree-holes for their nesting sites; so places like this, where streams flow through old-growth forest, are perfect for them. The mandarins, the wooden bridge, the blossom; it is as if I have suddenly been transported to the Far East.

The tension breaks as the pair suddenly flush, with a clatter of wings that is enough to startle a group of nearby mallards into flight. The mandarins fly away but then reverse direction and fly back over my head, wheeling between the tree trunks. I lean on the railing of the bridge and watch as the fallen blackthorn petals drift towards me and under the bridge at my feet. And then I suddenly start. That is the wrong way; the stream is somehow flowing backwards. It takes me a while to realise that this is a kind of illusion. The waters are so slow-moving that even today's barely perceptible light breeze is enough to set the flotsam, and even the surface ripples, moving upstream against the flow.

I decide to leave the trail and set off into the woods and follow the course of the river. It is not easy going; there are many fallen trees to clamber over, there is much thick scrub of thorn and butcher's broom, and where the ground is clear it is often boggy, pocked and poached by the footprints of beasts that have come to drink at the river. The forest floor is dense with constellations of celandines and violets. The river twists and turns, divides and re-forms around little islands, and loops through the wood as if it is still looking for its way.

I surprise another mandarin drake almost at my feet and wait for it to take to the air in a panic, but instead it slips behind an overhanging bankside alder and hides itself in the scrub. The waters are reddish; having emerged from a valley mire on heathland, they are acidic and poor in nutrients, but nonetheless rich in life. The leaves of bog pondweed and even waterlilies float on the calm surface of the river in great patches, and there are marsh marigolds in flower on the water's edge, and stands of the sword-like leaves of yellow flag, a native iris. Later in the year the river will be buzzing with dragonflies and damselflies, trout will be running and kingfishers will be dashing upstream and down, always in a hurry to be somewhere else. There is a reason why this river is so dense with life; its route from its source at almost no point passes through agricultural land, so unlike just about any other river you could think of it is not troubled by fertiliser run-off, by pesticides or herbicides. You could probably drink straight from this river; its water might be peaty but it is clean.

Back out on the heath I finally see my first migrants. In an alder and willow brake that follows a little stream as it winds lazily along the valley bottom, I see a familiar red flash, the flicking tail of a redstart, or firetail as it was once called. And then a second bird nearby; they have already paired up and claimed their territory. This is one of our most beautiful birds, I always think, and one that I have a long history with; I surveyed them in the woods of Wales, modified nest boxes for them, held them in my hands and ringed their young. I will always have an abiding affection for them.

In a stand of furze out on the heath, a small bird is hiding deep in the bushes. As I approach it slips away, into the next bush, and the next. At first I think it must be a Dartford warbler, a scarce resident warbler that is a local speciality, and lives almost exclusively amongst the furze on these lowland heaths. This bird is well known for doing just this; leading you on through the undergrowth and then losing you, like a will-o'-the-wisp. But when I finally catch up with this bird, I see that it is a newly arrived migrant, a whitethroat, my first warbler of the year, fresh from a journey across the Sahara. The migrants have finally come. Spring is here at last.

SIX

The Value of Everything

April 2019

It is something of an historical curiosity that for a country that is one of the most deforested in Europe, Britain is so well supplied with truly ancient trees, and in fact has more ancient oaks than the whole of the rest of Europe put together. The greatest concentration of these is in the New Forest, where more than a thousand trees have been identified as ancient, over four or five hundred years old. Most of these survivors are oak, but there are also good numbers of huge and venerable beech trees. The long-term survival of these trees is perhaps largely an accidental by-product of the Norman propensity for deer hunting. All those deer forests and deer parks scattered across the country have served to protect their trees from exploitation, by default more than by good intentions. Some of these trees may also have had their lives extended through pollarding – lopping off the tops to promote the growth of side branches – and you can see in an old oak where this has been the case: a massive trunk with a low crown and heavy branches radiating in all directions.

Some of the most imposing trees in the forest come with their own associated legends and have been given names and may even be marked on the maps; the Knightwood Oak, for instance, or the Eagle Oak, where supposedly the last eagle in the forest was shot. Not that this is something to brag about, I would have thought. This tree was already a giant then, and has waited for more than two centuries for the eagles to return; it seems that may finally be a possibility, as sea-eagles have recently been reintroduced to the south coast after a long, long absence. But today I have come to see an oak that, so far as I know, has no name, one that I stumbled upon myself on a visit a few years ago.

It is nearly the end of April, almost two weeks since I was last here, and the forest has transformed. The enclosures are carpeted with bluebells and the bracken is emerging, and the trees are all in leaf. The beech leaves are a pale lemony green, and the oak leaves are ringed with red. There is a freshness to all the new growth that is invigorating. The blackthorn blossom is coming to an end, and being replaced by the may blossom, the hawthorn, with its musky scent that rockets me straight back to childhood. The woods are full of birdsong, a cuckoo is calling relentlessly in the distance, and the woodpeckers are drumming.

I say that I came upon this old oak by myself, but that's not entirely true. I was out on Balmer Lawn near Brockenhurst, admiring some splendid old solitary oaks, when a passing couple told me that if I wanted to see the mother of them all I should take a look in that copse over there. There is something about the air in the forest that makes strangers talk to each other. This was a few years ago now, the only time since childhood that I had more than a passing visit here. I was on a writing deadline and I decided to book a few days in a B&B in Brockenhurst and stick at it until the work was done. Inevitably, I spent more time than I should have walking, following kingfishers along the streams and watching roe deer deep in the woods. I don't know what I was thinking, that I would be able to come to a place like this and spend my time indoors.

The tree is in the very centre of the little copse, in a sunlit grassy glade. It is as if the other trees have moved away, to give her space, out of respect. She is massive, with a huge gnarled trunk, and branches as big as most of the other trees in the wood. She reminds me of the matriarch of a herd of elephants, surrounded by her children and grandchildren. She has her first flush of pale wrinkled leaves, a strange combination of the ephemeral and the timeless. I could climb this tree, I think, it would be easy, she is all handholds. But I won't, for it would seem somehow inappropriate. Instead, I just place my hand on her wrinkled bark, like a handshake. A robin is hopping in the bushes nearby, watching me, and suddenly bursts into song.

It is perhaps understandable why people can feel such a powerful sense of affinity or attachment to a tree such as this. While almost all members of a species of plant or animal are virtually indistinguishable to us, a tree in its prime grows to become unlike any other. It is no wonder that we become tempted to ascribe to them what seems like an individual personality, an essence all their own.

Just a few yards away is a large shallow pond, lit up

with flowers and fringed with a scrub of thorn, and I walk over to take a closer look. As I approach, a party of goldfinches flies up from where they had been drinking at the water's edge. The pool is almost completely over-grown with water-crowfoot, a buttercup of the waters. The flowers stand proud of the floating leaves, white petalled but with a brilliant golden heart. There are thousands of them sparkling in the sunlight; it is like looking at a constellation of twinkling stars. This is probably the common water-crowfoot, but this family of plants is large and complicated, containing many very similar species, and it takes expert knowledge, if not genetic testing, to recognise them all with complete confidence. One of them, *Ranunculus novae-forestae*, is a local speciality. The New Forest water-crowfoot is a hybrid between two other less common species that is endemic to the forest. I could be looking at a plant that is found nowhere else but here, and I would never know.

I set out across the lawn, a wide expanse of closely cropped grassland studded with solitary trees and small copses. It looks almost like the African savannah in the sunshine, helped by the large numbers of grazing ponies dotted everywhere. They are particularly numerous in places like this, where the soil is rich enough to support grass rather than heath. I am headed to the far side of the lawn, to a place with the splendid name of Standing Hat. The forest is full of places with names that are charmingly odd: Anthony's Bee Bottom; Rakes Brakes Bottom; Little Stubby Hat; Brown Loaf; Burnt Balls; Ragged Boys Hill; Freeworms Hill; Mouse's Cupboard. And then there are other names that just trip off the tongue: Winding Stonard; Bagnum Bog; Burnt Axon; the Noads; Upper Lazy Bushes; Tantany Wood; Gurnetfields Furzebrake; Costicles Inclosure. Every name must tell a story, but the story has often been long forgotten, and all that is left is a name on a map, and the imagination. I gather up these place names as I roam about the forest, and store them in my commonplace book, as if I were collecting pressed flowers.

In the hilly copses of Standing Hat, I come upon a shallow muddy pool, with islands in its middle overgrown with sallow bushes. Above the surface of the water, flowers of bogbean are standing proud. This is another local speciality, a characteristic plant of the forest pools. Its flower spikes have pinkish-red buds and beautiful white feathery flowers. This is a plant worth seeking out.

I want to take a photograph of them, to preserve them in memory, but I have no camera save for that in my phone, and cannot get close enough. They are too far out from the edge, and will just be flowery dots in the distance.

The forest is renowned not only for its rare plants and birds, but also for its invertebrates. Although it is still early for many species of butterfly, orange-tips are flitting around the edge of the copses. Only the male has that brilliant orange splash on its white wings, but both male and female have a delicate mossy green tracery on their underwing. Butterflies have always been a feature of the forest. Well over a hundred years ago, W. H. Hudson was complaining about the hordes of collectors that would descend on the forest each year, at a time when entomology, even more than ornithology, was based on the central premise of catch-and-kill. Many species are holding out here that have spiralled into a seemingly terminal decline elsewhere, and the same applies to the dragonflies and damselflies. These are creatures of the summer months, but I see my first of the year, a large red damselfly. I shall seek out some of the more elusive species on my later visits, and perhaps also keep my eye out for Britain's only cicada, the New Forest cicada. I am hardly optimistic; its call is too high-pitched for me to hear, or in fact for most people to hear, so I will have my work cut out, although Hudson was one of the lucky few and was able to describe its call all those years ago. It has also not been seen for twenty years. It is probably extinct, but cicadas are renowned for disappearing for years at a time, as part of a life cycle that sees them spend most of their lives underground, only to all suddenly emerge together. Enthusiasts are still holding on to the possibility that in some remote unvisited woodland glade there may still be an unknown colony waiting to be rediscovered, and to that end there have even been recording devices secreted in likely locations through the forest, in the hope of catching one in song. I would like to think they are still hiding here somewhere, for their loss would not just be the loss from Britain of another species, but of our only representative of an entire family, another step towards the relentless depletion of our world.

Just recently, a colony of another rather charismatic insect, the mole cricket, was found in the New Forest, having been thought extinct in Britain for decades. There have been a few scattered records over the years, but these have all been thought to have emerged from imported compost or pot plants. Britain is one of the most well-watched and well-studied places in the world when it comes to natural history. It is remarkable to think that there may still be animals and plants in forgotten corners of our woods and hills that have managed to escape our attention, and of whose lives we remain completely ignorant.

It is the large, visible plants and animals – the trees, the birds, the mammals – that inevitably garner most of our attention, but we do well not to neglect the smaller things in life, that all have their place in the scheme of things. As the American writer Jon Mooallem put it: Maybe you have to believe in the value of everything to believe in the value of anything. The continuity of this forest, and its great range of habitats, make it a great reservoir of life; for lichens and fungi, for flowering plants and invertebrates. Another notable resident of the forest is a small crustacean called the triop, *Triops cancriformis*, which, as its name suggests, is a three-eyed wonder. It looks very much like a miniature horseshoe crab the size of a shrimp, and is sometimes also known as the tadpole shrimp. Until another colony was more recently found in Scotland, it was known in Britain only from a single pond here in the New Forest. And not just any pond, but a seasonal pond, that would flood briefly and then dry out for the remainder of the year. The triop has to race through its life cycle in a few short weeks before its world disappears around it, and then lives on only as eggs in the dried-out mud, waiting for the rains. It may seem like a precarious and horribly vulnerable way to make a living, but it evidently works, for fossil evidence shows that the triop genus has been around for as much as three hundred and sixty million years, since the dawn of the carboniferous period, long before the time of the dinosaurs, before the break-up of Pangaea, or indeed before the formation of Pangaea. Continents have risen and fallen, multiple mass extinction events have wiped out most life on earth, and always, some-where in a muddy puddle, has been a triop. That something so short-lived can be so long-lived is a thing of beauty, I think.

There is a fine stand of beeches here, with a charac-teristic bare forest floor beneath. Some of the beeches in the New Forest are almost of an age with the oldest of the oak trees. Oak and beech are the most emblematic trees of these grazed woodlands, but one other forms a constant part of the mix – the holly. Most of them are just bushes, able to grow because their prickles offer them some protection against grazing, and indeed we tend to think of them as shrubs rather than proper trees, a part of the understory only. But given the chance, they can keep going and reach their full potential. Walking in the woods south of Beaulieu Road, I had come upon a couple of giants, relatively speaking. Their trunks were perhaps three feet across, and they were thirty or forty feet high. Their dense canopy of leaves was almost entirely smooth and without spines. Even if you look at a holly bush you will see that the prickles are concentrated on the lower leaves, while those uppermost leaves, out of the reach of grazers, have no need to resort to them. These defences are contingent. The two full-grown hollies I had come upon could have been as much as five hundred years old. There is something that feels deeply reassuring about being among ancient trees: the sense of a deeper time. It is comforting to think that there are living things that were around long before us, and will persist long after we are gone. It speaks to our hope for the future, that no matter how hard we try to fuck absolutely everything up, there is a life that will somehow make it through to the other side.

I step through a gate into the enclosures at the edge of the lawn, and walk along a broad woodland ride. There are bluebells beneath the trees, and dog violets and the lemony-green florets of wood spurge along the grassy verge. Speckled wood butterflies are everywhere, bold and battling for territory. And then I spot a less familiar butterfly. As it perches, I see its underwing, a mosaic of white and pale orange and rusty-red patches ringed in black. The light shines through it like a stained-glass window. It is a pearl-bordered fritillary, a creature I have never knowingly seen before. I had heard this area of the woods was known for them, and in fact is specifically managed for their benefit, but it is early; they do not usually fly until May. They used to be relatively widespread across the country, haunting the coppices that were their preferred habitat, but then coppicing was virtually dropped from the repertoire of woodland management a century or so ago, and they were left homeless, falling into a catastrophic decline. They are now extremely local, in England at least, and even here in the New Forest have held on in only a few favoured locations.

Deeper in the woods, I step away from the ride to follow a narrow stream, little more than a winding ditch. My map tells me that it is called Etherise Gutter. One for the notebook. Perhaps this is forestese for sleepy hollow, I think – that would make sense. The stream leads me down to the Lymington River, and then I can follow a lane back to Brockenhurst, for I have one more destination in mind. I want to pay a visit to the oldest tree in the forest. But on my way I am distracted by a little bird flitting about in a holly bush. At first I assume it is a warbler, perhaps a willow warbler, and nearly walk straight past. I am constantly seeing little birds from the corner of my eye that disappear into the undergrowth before I have got a proper look at them. This is one of the unspoken secrets of watching birds; that half the birds you see are up and gone before you've had the chance to make a confident identification. You just don't mention all the ones that got away. I am assuming this is true of everybody, and is not just a reflection of inadequate skills on my part. This bird is different, though; every time it hops from branch to branch it stays in full view. Every time. It has a bandit mask and a splash of brilliant orange for a little feathered cap. It is a firecrest – a male, for the female's cap is buttercup yellow rather than orange. Along with its much commoner relative the goldcrest, it is the very smallest of our birds, smaller even than the wren. And like the goldcrest, it can apparently be astonishingly bold. One might call it confiding, but it is more that, unlike most small birds, which are timid and flighty, it is simply indifferent to me. It is just not bothered whether I am there or not. Perhaps it is a matter of scale; the threats it faces are much smaller and faster-moving than I am, in the same way that bugs will largely just ignore us. Indifferent nature feels like an honour; you get so used to living creatures vanishing over the horizon at the first whiff of us, and treating us like the monstrous predator that we possibly are.

The first British breeding record for the firecrest was back in the sixties, here in the forest, and since then it has become a regular breeder, though still in small numbers – hundreds of birds rather than thousands. About half of these are in its heartland in the New Forest. It was not a bird I thought I had much chance of seeing, for it is tiny and is scattered through the forest, mostly in the deep cover of the stands of conifer where it prefers to make its home. I was not particularly planning to go out looking for them, but one came to me anyway.

The parish church of St Nicholas is beautifully situated, on a hilltop overlooking the village. It is the oldest church in the forest. Although some parts of it are later Victorian additions, much of it is Norman, and there are elements that are Saxon. The church predates the Norman invasion a thousand years ago, predates the New Forest itself as an identifiable entity. There are even suggestions that the hill on which it sits may be partly artificial, and that the church was built on an existing sacred site, a pagan temple perhaps. Right beside the church is its churchyard yew. Most yews, not just these solitaries but those in yew woodland such as those at Butser Hill in Hampshire, or Kingley Vale in West Sussex, are broad and low, their massive branches even reaching down to touch the ground around them. But this tree is tall, taller even than the top of the church spire, though admittedly this is no Salisbury Cathedral. Its massive trunk is ribbed, with each rib the breadth of a decent-sized tree trunk. It looks rather like a whole copse of trees that have been bound together into a giant faggot. Or like an enormous candle that has melted and then solidified. As I did with the old oak tree earlier, I place my hand on its trunk, which has a girth of perhaps twenty feet; there is something awe-inspiring about such trees, the sense they give of being a living embodiment of deep time. This tree has been dated and found to be over a thousand years old, twice the age of the oldest of the giant oaks. Generations of trees have fallen in the forest, and perhaps forty generations of people have lived, loved, worked and died, and this tree has just kept right on growing.

I don't go into the church, but before I leave I take a walk around the graveyard to pay my respects. I like churchyards; I know that some people find them gloomy, but I always think of them as somehow reassuring, that we are all part of the same cycle, that we are all in this together. There are war graves here, for commonwealth soldiers who were treated in field hospitals locally but never made it home. History, history.

SEVEN

Pern

May 2019

The New Forest is sufficiently large that I could easily fill a book with walks whose paths never once crossed. But it doesn't quite seem to ever work out that way; I keep finding myself stumbling onto spots that have a certain special appeal, and thinking to myself: Wow, what a lovely place this is, I must come back here when the spring has come, when the migrants have arrived, at a different time of day, when I have longer before I have to rush back for the train, and so on. The truth is that I am not ultimately really interested in walking as an activity, as exercise or as challenge; walking is primarily a means of getting to a place where I want to be. Though it does seem that the best way to immerse yourself in a landscape is at the pace of a slow walk, with frequent pauses. The goal is not to walk through a landscape, but to walk into it. The point of a walk is not to reach the end, but to reach the middle. To find the centre of things, and soak it all in. When I walk I am empty-headed, alert and attentive, absorbing the world around me, my focus entirely outwards. But when I come to reflect on the walk I have just taken, I find myself thinking about all the things I could have thought, but didn't, and the memory of the walk becomes a conversation with myself.

It is an occasional fantasy of mine that one day, after a lifetime of roaming, I will finally reach a spot where I think: This is it, this is perfect, there is no need for me ever to move again. The fear is that what had seemed perfect one day might seem wanting the next. There will always be something that I miss. I love the shoreline, but I love the mountains too; I love the deep forest, but sometimes I yearn for the bleak austerity of a desert. I can never have everything that I want, all in one place, all in one time, and so I suspect that I am destined to keep on wandering.

I came upon this clearing on one of my previous walks, and knew at once that it was somewhere I would have to come back to. It is hard to define exactly what qualities I am looking for that have this particular appeal to my sense of belonging. It was a large grassy clearing, with an enclosure of mostly conifers to one side, and open wood pasture of oak on the other, with a stream winding through it. The clearing rose and fell in little hillocks, a mix of grass and heather and bracken. It was studded with Scots pine trees and a maze of furze bushes, full of hidden corners where you could lose yourself. And so I paused a while, gave up on any vague plans I might have had of getting somewhere else, and drank it in. You notice more when you stop moving too; it may feel that you have a greater chance of seeing things worth seeing the more ground you cover, but this is a false economy. It is time rather than distance that is needed to take in as much as possible of what nature has to offer, and the stiller and quieter you are then the less impact you have on your surroundings. After a short while a little bird flew right over my head, stumpy like a miniature rocket, crossing the clearing from side to side. A hawfinch, a bird that is not easy to see, for it tends to stay in the very tops of the trees, and which I had missed seeing at its winter roosts on my earlier visits. Then a much larger bird dropped from its perch in a pine at the edge of the clearing and began to fly low along the wall of conifers. The most striking thing about it was the glare of its brilliant white under-tail coverts. At first it was relatively leisurely in flight, but then it instantly switched gear, and suddenly accelerated away at tremendous speed, as though it had engaged jets. A hunting goshawk. It was incredible that this bird could suddenly generate such propulsive force. I watched as it raced along the forest wall, but it was lost to view before I could make out its target.

I have come back to revisit this clearing on a sunny May afternoon. I choose a spot in the very centre of the open ground, with a wide view, but sheltered by a little group of Scots pines. I brush away the fallen cones from the grass beneath the trees, and sit back, and wait. The wait is not a long one. Almost at once the fuzz-jacks emerge from the nearby furze bushes; it is as though there is a pair for every clump. I don't tire of their constant accompaniment as they bounce around me; they are lovely little birds and so ever-present that they are starting to feel like my own personal retinue. Swallows sweep around the edges of the clearing; they have been notably late this year, and few in number, and there has been concern over what might be happening somewhere on their long migration. It is good to have them here. I try not to play favourites, but some creatures make it hard not to. It is the sheer gracefulness of a swallow in flight that I find irresistible, and suffice to say that I have had a tattoo of a swallow on my shoulder since I was a teenager. This was back in the days before body art was much recognised as an art at all, and in fact was still faintly disreputable. The choice of designs was vanishingly small, and the clientele primarily sailors. For the sailor, the swallow, returning every year to the very same barn, symbolised a safe homecoming. This year, there are too many empty barns, too many ships that have not come in.

A buzzard is circling lazily low above the clearing in the sunshine, and then a second begins to fly across the open ground at the height of the treetops. But I know instantly that there is a wrongness about it. Birdwatchers use the word *jizz* to describe the distinctive feel of a bird, that will sometimes enable them to see what is little more than a dot in the distance, and know at once what it is. It is as though each bird has its own individual character, based on general shape, flight pattern and, somehow, personality, that you absorb through long observation and by paying close attention. I have spent enough time watching buzzards to know at once that, though this may look a lot like one, it is decidedly something other. I look more closely, try to evaluate what is different about it; I am aided in this by the fact that there is an actual buzzard soaring usefully overhead for comparison. Although this bird is silhouetted against the sky, so it is hard to see its markings in any detail, its tail is a little too long, its head a little too small, and most of all, its mode of flight is just not the same. A buzzard will soar with its wings in a V-shape, and flap its wings above its back. This bird soars with its wings level, and flaps them down. It is a honey buzzard, my first. It is a deeply memorable moment. This, I think, is why some birdwatchers will go all out to track down rarities; it is not simply an urge to collect, for there is an undeniable thrill about that first glimpse of something new. It imprints itself on the mind, a frozen moment that almost seems to divide the relentless passage of life into a before and an after.

The honey buzzard is a notoriously elusive bird; certainly here, and even in other parts of Europe where it is more at home and much more numerous. It is a late migrant, not arriving until well into May, and less than fifty pairs breed here each year, in scattered locations, in Scotland and Wales, in north, south, east and west. More than that, its habits render it peculiarly inconspicuous. In his book *Raptor*, James Macdonald Lockhart travelled the length and breadth of Britain in search of all fifteen species of British breeding birds of prey, and the honey buzzard was the one bird that eluded him. He came here to the forest in search of them; it is probably the most reliable place for them, as a few pairs come here each summer. Their breeding locations are closely guarded secrets; there is just one site, at Acres Down near Lyndhurst, which is well known for sightings. People gather there to look for them from a viewpoint, to add them to their year-lists, or their life-lists, though even there many walk away disappointed. I had considered a visit there myself in the next month or so, once all the birds would definitely have arrived. It makes me happier, though, to stumble upon one by accident rather than by design; it seems somehow more natural, less contrived. More like an unexpected gift than a shopping trip.

The honey buzzard, despite its obvious similarities, is not all that close a relative of the true buzzards. It is a less robust bird, and it is thought that it may have evolved to resemble its distant cousin by way of Batesian mimicry, to afford it some protection against predation by the goshawk, which will hunt and kill most smaller birds of prey, but may show a little caution with a sturdy buzzard. Nor does the honey buzzard eat honey; rather it specialises predominantly in wasp grubs, of all things. So its name is a kind of flailing around in the right general direction, but never quite getting there. I rather like its alternative name; the pern. The pern sits quietly in a tree deep in the woods and waits for a passing wasp, which it will track back to its nest. It will create a mental map of all the nests in its territory, and when the time is right it will start digging. It may return to the same nest day after day until it is finally picked clean. Rather than the curved, grasping talons of most predatory birds, it has straight claws for walking about on the forest floor, and for digging. It has a small, hooked bill perfect for winkling grubs out of their comb one by one, and its head is covered in tiny, densely packed feathers that form a shield affording some protection against wasp stings.

This peculiar specialism makes its habitat requirements rather particular; it needs a place where wasps are plentiful, and it needs sandy or friable soil that is suitable for digging. This is why, in Britain at least, it is found only in a few scattered locations.

I can imagine the pern right now, deep in the woods, a waspish black-and-yellow eye in the foliage, peering out from amidst the dappled light of the canopy, looking intently for the slightest sign of movement, patiently awaiting a passing wasp, then setting off in silent, secretive pursuit. Hopefully it has found a mate and has begun to build its nest, in the most hidden recesses of the forest. Perhaps I will see it again sometime, if I am very lucky. I wish it happy hunting.

Time has run away with me; I have spent too long in my clearing in the woods. It is an hour back to the nearest railway station, and the train is in less than an hour. It will be many hours before the next train if I miss it; I am expected back, and I am not equipped for an overnight stay. I must kick myself into gear and strike out, through woods and heaths. Out on the open heath, both skylarks and woodlarks are singing, but I have no time to stop and give them their due.

The path I am following is leading me too far in the wrong direction; it looked right but the further I go the more it veers away, until it reaches the point where every step I take leads me further from where I need to be, rather than closer. I decide to abandon the trail, and strike out across the heath. At first it is fine, but soon I find myself in a boggy hollow of willow scrub and bog myrtle, and tussocky moor grass. I step from tussock to tussock; they wobble beneath my feet. A snipe fires up from my feet, cryptic and mottled, and jinks away into the distance. My foot slips and I find myself going down, down, down, until my leg is knee deep in bog water. I try to haul myself out and my other foot slides in too, so that I am now effectively thigh deep in a bog pond. I am right in the middle of a mire, hidden among the long grasses, and the only way out is to wade. I seem to have a remarkable talent for getting myself into this kind of ridiculous predicament. Looking around me, trying to find my most plausible way out, I notice that I am in the middle of a fine stand of flowering bogbeans; I even get out my phone to take a close-up photo. They are very beautiful, and I think to myself: Why not? Fretting about my predicament will not make me any drier. When I make my train, it will be with squelching shoes and jeans sodden with peaty water, and I will be soaked through for the three-hour journey. People will look at me from the corners of their eyes, will move their children away from me, will sit as far from me as is humanly possible. It bothers me a little, but in truth, not really all that much.

EIGHT

The Circle of Life

June 2019

On the heaths where I have been spending much of my time, the most visible birds have been the meadow pipits, larks and fuzz-jacks, but here in the heaths of the far south of the forest, I seem to have arrived in linnet country; they are everywhere. I cannot immediately see anything different in the habitat, but there must be something; the acidity of the soil must be different, or the balance of heather and grass, or the dominant species of grass. It is not just linnets either, but seed-eaters all round. Close to the pinewoods are siskins and redpolls, in the gorse brakes are parties of goldfinches and bullfinches, and at the edges of the oak woods are the inevitable chaffinches; I am pleased to see my first greenfinch here.

It may seem odd to be happy to see a bird that I would once have seen every day, but the greenfinch is no longer as commonplace as it once was. A parasitic disease called trichomonosis has arrived, spread, it is thought, largely through bird-feeders. It causes their throats to swell so that they can no longer swallow, and they starve to death in the midst of an abundance of food. We are killing them with kindness. Their population has been devastated. I spot a pair of yellowhammers, another bird that was a continuous presence during my childhood, but is now in steep decline and has been red-listed. As with so many of our farmland birds, it has been badly affected by agricultural changes. And in the mire and thick vegetation at a stream's edge I flush a reed bunting from her nest. I back swiftly away, splashing through the sodden moss. After my last visit, I have come slightly better prepared, and am wearing wellies.

Out on the heath a kestrel is hovering. They are not all that numerous here, because the small mammals that are their preferred prey are also only present in low densities. The heavy grazing means that there is not the thick ground layer that voles and mice prefer. In fact, apart from the deer, the forest is not all that generously supplied with mammals. The acid soils mean fewer earthworms available for shrews and hedgehogs, so these are not plentiful here. Even badgers rely heavily on earthworms to eat, and are also a little less numerous than you might expect. Squirrels are the most common mammals here, then rabbits, though even those are much less frequently seen than they were before myxomatosis, which was first brought to Britain in the 1950s. Weasels rely mainly on small mammals for their prey, and stoats on rabbits, and foxes on both, though they perhaps do a little better as they are more adaptable. Predators survive well here if they can turn to birds for their needs. Buzzards, which elsewhere will feed on rabbits and even earthworms, have crows as their most common food item. The kestrel on the heath is probably more likely to catch a pipit than a vole. One family of small mammal thrives spectacularly well, however – bats. Almost all British species are found here, including some great rarities, such as the barbastelle and the Bechstein's.

In all my visits to the forest I have seen just one fox, and that was a freshly killed one, lying in the middle of the road. Yet when I get home to the inner-city council estate where I live with my daughters in an old tenement block, it is odds on that I will see one there, for they are constant visitors. Neighbours regularly hand-feed them; if they offer them a tempting morsel of food, the foxes may even allow a cautious stroke, though this is perhaps not to be recommended. They have been transformed from country-dwellers to townies, much like most of us. It is my hope that one day I may once again live in a place where I can step out of my front door and straight into nature, but for the time being I shall have to make do with the foxes, fox-trotting along a brick wall at dusk, nose to the ground, in search of a tasty treat. And there are not only foxes in the city. In winter I can regularly watch the starlings gathering in their thousands to murmurate. I often see sparrowhawks circling over the estate. There are pied and grey wagtails, and winter blackcaps. Walking home from the library with my daughter, I spot a peregrine soaring right above us, and point it out to her. Nobody else has stopped; nobody else seems to have noticed it. I tell my daughter that it is the fastest bird in the world, that it has been timed in a dive at over two hundred miles per hour. She is impressed. I have watched this bird from my balcony, stooping on an unsuspecting pigeon; it was heart-stopping.

The New Forest is an environment that is depleted in some forms of life, but incredibly rich in others. Besides being a haven for many species of birds and rare flowering plants, there are other highlights that might escape the casual observer. The continuity and persistence of primary forest, with an abundance of fallen trees, means that this is the best place in Britain for the entire community of invertebrates that rely on dead wood, such as the spectacular stag beetle, now in steep decline in much of the country. The forest is home to more than four hundred species of beetle, and two hundred species of fly, whose life cycle is entirely dependent on fallen wood. And above our heads, above the reach of grazers, is a whole other world; just as in the rainforest, the greatest diversity of life is up in the canopy, rich with plants and animals that never touch the ground. This forest is home to the richest community of lichens anywhere in Europe. There are hundreds of species up there, many found hardly anywhere else other than in the New Forest, and some of them new to science, discovered during surveys in the past few years, and recorded nowhere else but here. Lichens are slow to disperse; even the oak woods planted hundreds of years ago may be relatively poorly supplied with them compared to the pasture woods that have been wooded continuously since the retreat of the glaciers.

And yet while this landscape has been to some extent shaped by man over the course of hundreds, if not thousands, of years, land management need not necessarily be hostile to nature. In her book *Braiding Sweetgrass*, Robin Wall Kimmerer looks at the relationship between people and plants, and comes to reconcile her scientific training as a botanist and her cultural understanding of plants as a member of the Potawatomi Nation. In examining the decline of sweetgrass, traditionally gathered by indigenous people of America, she found it still had healthy populations close to the reservations where it continued to be used, but was dying out where it was left untouched. The native tradition was only to crop no more than half of what was found, and to leave the rest for the future. By experiment, she showed that, if was left uncropped, colonies would become choked and would die out, but constant thinning caused them to thrive with continual fresh growth. It stands to reason that plants that have evolved alongside grazers might benefit from grazing pressure. Of course, if we adopt a culture where, each time we find a new resource, we dive in and use it all up mercilessly, then the story will be very different.

One of the groups of animals that particularly thrive here is the *Odonata* – the dragonflies and damselflies – of which almost three quarters of species known to Britain breed in the New Forest. It is due to the wide diversity of wetland habitats: the fast- and slow-running streams; the boggy mires and seeps; the heathland pools and the woodland ponds. These are creatures that only emerge as adults during the long hot days of summer, and summer seems to be running a little late this year. I head to a stream on the heath that is a well-known site, sit on the bankside and wait, but none seem to be forthcoming, not yet. At least I have the calls of the curlews around me to lift my spirits. Finally, I spot some, where the trail crosses a seep that is not even marked on the map, and a small pool has formed. The water is visibly healthy, filled with tadpoles and pondweed, and broad-bodied chasers are skimming the surface. A stumpy, dull-coloured female is laying her eggs, one by one. She dips her tail into the water and delicately plants each egg onto pondweed that lies just beneath the surface. Above her hovers an azure-bodied male, guarding her. He darts away to drive off another male that approaches a little too close. They seem to lead a life of relentless skirmishes. Then I spot a tiny, needle-thin damselfly – a small red, a rare species that is a speciality of the forest. That is my lot for the day, but I am satisfied.

I am worried for the birds. There has been an awful lot of rain this June. I cannot help but recall many years ago, when I managed a whole woodland's worth of nest boxes, accommodating pied flycatchers and redstarts, blue, great, coal and marsh tits, and nuthatches. One year it rained throughout the month of June and the effect was catastrophic: perhaps eighty per cent of broods failed entirely, after the eggs had hatched rather than before. It was heartbreaking. The parent birds either couldn't find enough food to prevent the young from starving, or they spent so much time away from the nest searching that the young became chilled. But I am back in the forest for solstice day now, and the weather seems to have turned at last, and is dry and sunny. For the precise moment of the solstice, when the sun reaches its very northernmost point in the sky, I head to a favourite pool.

As I approach, there are family parties of redstarts in the trees and bushes. On the wooden rail where the trail crosses a mire are three fluffed-up fledgling fuzz-jacks – fuzz-balls, perhaps – and I wait and watch as their parents come to feed them. I feel reassured that this month has apparently not been a complete washout for the birds.

Over the pool, broad-bodied and four-spotted chasers are circulating, beating the bounds and conducting constant aerial battles; they seem to lead such complicated and inscrutable lives in the month or two they are on the wing. A pair of mallards, wary of my presence, lead a flotilla of ducklings across the water, and by the reeds a moorhen is shepherding her single youngster. At the water's edge a little egret is poised, brilliant white. These birds have only returned to Britain in the past couple of decades, and I still haven't entirely got used to them; they look somehow alien to me, tropical. Their rapid expansion in range may be partly due to milder weather, but perhaps more to a reduction in persecution. Hundreds of years ago they were common resident birds, but were relentlessly hunted, first for food, and finally for fashion; their elegant white plumes were so in demand for ladies' hats that they became almost extinct across the whole of Europe. It was groups of Victorian women protesting about the over-exploitation of birds for the trade in exotic feathers that led to the foundation of the Royal Society for the Protection of Birds.

I strike out through the woods and onto the heaths; the longest day warrants a long walk. My plan is to walk until darkness falls and then get the last train home. June is orchid month. On my visit earlier in the month I had searched and found just one solitary common spotted orchid. But now the heaths are lit up with them, hundreds upon hundreds of heath-spotted orchids. They vary hugely; some have white flowers patterned with delicate pink, while others are deep mauve with a tracery of the darkest purple. It is a show that I had not wanted to miss out on. Everything changes so fast; every time I pass a week without visiting, I start to wonder at all the sights I might have seen had I been more determined not to miss a thing.

I am crossing a wide flat heath, where the heather is short and stubby and interspersed with grassy patches, heavily grazed. Far off in the distance I can see a herd of fallow deer. I scope them out through my binoculars;

there are nineteen of them, all female, and one is pure white. Incredibly, it seems to be the exact same herd, unchanged, that I saw three months ago in March, and several miles away. It is like running unexpectedly into an old friend. The big skies over the heath seem bereft of birds, but then a woodlark launches from close by, hovers right above me on its unmistakable little round wings, and breaks into song. I have never been so close to one before. Two notes. Is that really all I get? Two notes.

The heath I am crossing may seem quiet and mostly birdless, but as I approach the woodland edge I can see a whole throng of them, in constant motion. Something is afoot. A dozen mistle thrushes launch themselves from the trees to the ground at the heathland edge, then almost immediately back to the trees, then again back to the ground. They are on edge; their heads jerk to left and right. Then a whole flock of smaller birds, scores of them, emerge from amongst the trees. It is as if they have been driven out by beaters. It seems extraordinary that such a small wood could hold so many birds. I can make out redstarts and robins, chaffinches and warblers, and others that I cannot confidently identify at this distance. They leave the trees but seem hesitant to fly far from cover. And they stay tight together, rather than breaking away and making a dash for it over open ground. It is unusual to see birds of different species flocking together, but this is clearly an act of necessity. They begin to circulate in a rolling mass, not horizontally but vertically, spinning like a Catherine wheel tight beside the trees.

Then, finally, I see him. A little male sparrowhawk races along the woodland edge and crashes through the centre of the roiling frenzy of birds, twisting and grabbing. But the birds have defeated him, by shoaling like fish. Perhaps a hundred birds, all in constant motion, blurring together so there is no one target to aim for. Safety in numbers. The sparrowhawk, empty-taloned, perches on the bough of an oak and begins to preen nonchalantly, as if to say: No bother, I wasn't all that hungry anyway. He is a handsome little predator, with a grey-blue back and a red-streaked breast. It strikes me that in my visits to the forest I have twice seen the scarce and elusive goshawk before I have seen my first sparrowhawk, generally a much commoner bird. The fact is that when the goshawk moves in then the number of sparrowhawks immediately declines. They either clear out or they are caught and killed. Predator becomes prey.

As dusk begins to approach a roe deer emerges onto the trail ahead of me, grazing casually on the grass between the oaks. I get nearer and keep expecting her to make a run for it, but she seems untroubled. The fallow deer always seem alert and skittish, but roe deer appear to be less concerned by the presence of man. Perhaps, as their numbers are lower, they are not so subject to culling, and have less reason to be fearful. Or perhaps it is just a matter of personality. I sit on a fallen log nearby and watch her for a while as she makes her slow unhurried progress through the stand of trees. She comes to a stream, a deep ditch, and decides to cross it. She bends all four legs at once and then straightens them suddenly, flying high into the air as though trampolining, far higher than was strictly necessary. I have never seen a deer jump like this before – I have seen antelopes leap similarly in Africa, where it is known as pronking, but never a deer. There is something joyful about it, as if she is jumping because she can, rather than because she needs to.

I would like to see more of the creatures of the night, but for that I am going to have make new plans. The last train leaves only about fifteen minutes after sunset. I take a final walk through a plantation of conifers as the light begins to fail. A little herd of fallow deer is suddenly on the ride ahead of me. I momentarily glance down at my feet to find my footing, and when I look up a moment later the deer have all melted away into invisibility. Otherwise, the air is still and there is no sign of life; as though the creatures are waiting for me to pass before coming out to play. But I cannot stop and wait; I have a train to catch.

NINE

The Man Who Loved Tractors

June 2019

Sitting in a beer garden in the sunshine, waiting for a pub lunch and watching the house martins racing in and out of their nests in the eaves. If I was on my own then stopping for food wouldn't have even crossed my mind; it would be a sandwich and a bottle of tap water out in the woods. Any time not spent out in the forest would be time wasted. But the summer is here, exams are over, and my daughters have been angling to see what I've been up to on my repeated expeditions. It seems that I am compelled to re-enact the family outings of my own childhood.

After we are all fed, we set off across the heath towards the woods. On the boardwalk over the mire the bog asphodels are in bloom; spikes of starry, yellow-orange flowers. I pluck a leaf of bog myrtle and get my girls to test the scent. It is common here, though in Britain it is more a plant of the Highlands. It is sweet and resinous, and familiar perhaps from mosquito repellents. Before the introduction of hops it was widely used to flavour beer, and still is very occasionally, in what is called gruit beer. It makes me think of Australia, too, for it is reminiscent of the scent of eucalyptus.

I introduce the girls to the heath-spotted orchid, and they approve. Orchids are an easy win, with their evident glamour. And then we begin to see little blue butterflies fluttering among the heather at our feet. The season has begun. These are the silver-studded blue, rather than the common blue, which was so much a feature of my childhood summers on the downs. The silver-studded blue is generally quite a scarce creature, but can be locally numerous where the conditions are just right, and here in the forest they are probably the most numerous butterflies of all. Anya gets out her camera, and we chase the little things about, trying to catch them settled. She has a photography project for school, and has brought a camera along specially, in the hope of getting some shots she can make good use of.

As with most of the blues, the silver-studded has a lifestyle of supreme complexity. It lays its eggs on heather stalks close to the nest of the black ant *Lasius niger*. Other blues choose other species of ants. When the caterpillars hatch, they produce a sweet secretion that the ants harvest, in return protecting the caterpillars from predators. And when the caterpillars pupate, the ants may even carry the chrysalises down into their nests and guard them there. The butterflies may emerge as imagos underground, in the midst of an ant colony. You could say that the ants are farming the butterflies, or that the butterflies are farming the ants. Life is not just about predation and competition and exploitation; it can be about cooperation and collaboration too. Not that there is any question of intent. Evolution can lead you down some strange byways; the only rule is that if it works it persists. I tell this story, the story of how this butterfly lives, to my daughters; I must admit that I am enjoying sharing some of the things that fascinate me. I like to think that the complexities of the natural world are intrinsically interesting, and the more you know then the more fascinating they become. My daughters may be at a stage in their lives when the most interesting things are clothes and parties, but I cannot help but hope that a little of my enthusiasm may rub off on them.

We reach the pasture woods and follow a trail along the woodland edge. Kaya, walking ahead, spots a wood mouse running across the path ahead of her. I miss it, probably with my head in the air looking for birds. She is closer to the ground than me, I tell myself. I like to speculate that I see far more when I am on my own, with my attention focused and undistracted, but I have to admit that ultimately this is just speculation, and is self-serving, a justification for the way I like to do things. I see what I see, but have no idea at all just how much I am missing. It could be that I am surrounded by wonders, and miss them all by constantly looking completely the wrong way.

Walking alongside the stands of bracken that flank the woods, my daughters jump back when they hear something beneath the bracken that I cannot hear. It sounds like a rattlesnake, they say. Now the New Forest may be home to all six species of reptile that we have in Britain, but none of them make a sound remotely like that of a rattlesnake. I suspect that they have come upon a wood cricket, a local speciality that is rare elsewhere.

There are several uncommon cricket and bush-cricket species that live here in the forest, and I want to ask the girls to show me where the sound is coming from so I can get a look at it, and see what they have found. But they have run away.

There is so much that I can no longer hear. These woods are full of willow warblers and wood warblers, but because I cannot hear them singing it is hard to track them down and to know where I should be looking for them. Perhaps there could be benefits to travelling with a hearing companion, the ears to my eyes, someone who could help point me in the right direction. Perhaps I should be urging my daughters to listen to birdsong recordings and to learn them for me. But they have more than enough to learn in life without me adding to it. An interest like that has to come from within.

It is said that introverts are people who are energised by time spent alone, and drained of energy by time spent in company. By this measure I would definitely qualify; while I may occasionally enjoy social events, I always end up finding myself looking forward to the time when I can return to my natural state, and unwind on my own. But my children are the exception to this.

It could be the result of long familiarity, or it could be that, not consciously but psychologically, I perceive them as being not entirely separate from me, almost a partial projection of myself into the future. Though, of course, a big part of the story of growing up is the assertion of your own, individual, unique personality, independent of your parents. Certainly, in my teenage years I defined my identity almost entirely in opposition to my father; if he thought something, then I thought the opposite. I suspect that this conflict may have been a driving force behind many of the choices I have made in life.

When most of my friends were taking their driving tests, I made a very deliberate decision not to learn to drive a car. My rationale was environmental: there was too much pollution in the world, being produced by too many cars, and the overwhelming majority of vehicles on the road at any one time had seats for at least four people but had just one individual sitting in them. I would hitch-hike, or take public transport, or ride a motorbike instead. Bikes were less harmful, I convinced myself, and also cooler. It was very much a line in the sand, however. I am sure my father's whole sense of identity centred around cars. It was not just his skill as a mechanic, and that he spent most of his spare time tinkering with them. When I was still young he would be out driving in off-road trials most weekends, and while he indulged my constant craving to visit nature reserves, I am sure he would rather have been at Goodwood. Later in life he would take annual trips to Le Mans and exhibit his cars at shows. He made a point of always owning cars that would turn people's heads; often enough they would be his own mutant creations. A unique car was a sign that you had made it in life. Why would you spend your money on something that was invisible, such as a holiday, when you could spend it on something that all the world could see? I would slump down in the back seat; the last thing you want as a fourteen-year-old is for everybody to be looking at you and pointing.

We are all, in part at least, a product of our environment. My father's family had, he said, been the first in his street to own a car. The day it arrived, they drove it up and down the road while all the neighbours came out to admire it. The car, to him, was a statement, one that I conspicuously rejected. I hope that I have brought up my own children in sufficiently relaxed a way that they don't feel compelled to systematically reject my values, one by one. To be fair, they are almost grown now and still seem quite content to indulge me.

We pass through a gate, from the open-pasture woodland to the enclosures. The trees, a mix of conifers and broadleaves, are not so ancient here, and are less widely spaced. The fencing keeps out the livestock but is not tall enough to defeat the deer, so these woods are not entirely ungrazed. But the grass grows thick on the narrower rides, though the main thoroughfares are gravelled. There is a dense shrub layer of thorn and bramble and honeysuckle. In sunny spots are the great mounded nests of wood ants, with trails leading from them out to the nearby trees. It is extraordinary that an animal so small can leave such a trail, but that is the power of numbers. A wood ant mound is an ant city; it can house up to four hundred thousand individuals. This is a keystone species, with a huge impact on its environment. It protects the trees, by keeping down the numbers of all the invertebrates that feed on them. Without them, these trees might find themselves stripped of leaves by caterpillars. And the nests themselves are microhabitats of their own; there are species of beetle and woodlouse and other ants that are found nowhere else, and are completely dependent on them. I explain these things to my daughters, but trying to get them to show interest in ants is a step too far.

A butterfly comes swinging down the ride towards us and I point it out. It is a silver-washed fritillary, my first of the year. It is the largest of our several fritillary species, big and almost birdlike in flight with its long, pointed wings. In the next few weeks the butterfly season will be at its peak, and the dragonfly season too, just as most birds are going into moult and becoming harder to spot.

My daughters are telling me a joke, a very long joke, taking turns as if in a tag team. It is the tale of the man who loved tractors, one of those rambling shaggy-dog stories that can be constantly adapted and added to with barely relevant details, all in service to an endlessly deferred punchline. I have the feeling that I have heard this joke before, but for the life of me can't remember where it is going.

There once was a man who loved tractors. He really loved tractors. He had a huge collection of toy tractors and model tractors, he had a huge library of books about classic tractors of the world, and on the walls of his house, where people sometimes keep portraits of their ancestors, he had framed photos and paintings of his very favourite, beautiful tractors. He waited impatiently each Friday for his copy of *Farm Machinery Weekly*, even though, to his mind, it had rather too much to say about threshers and combine harvesters, which weren't the same thing at all. His idea of a good day was going to a country fair and watching the tractor racing, and for his holidays he would save up to go to the Tractorland theme park.

I stop in my tracks. Shush a minute, I say. Ahead of us beneath the overarching trees a pair of fallow deer are crossing the ride. They haven't seen us yet. Their white-spotted summer coats are markedly conspicuous when they are out in the open, but here in the dappled sunshine beneath the canopy the point of them becomes immediately apparent, for they blend in almost magically with the pattern of light and shadow, and you can see just why they would lose their spots in winter. Of course they would. They graze a little on the grass of the ride and then drift on into the trees.

The man who loved tractors had a wife, and he loved

her too, though he couldn't understand why she didn't share his interest. One day he went out for a drive in his car, and came home a few hours later riding a shiny new tractor. What have you done? said his wife. How am I supposed to go shopping in that? This time you've gone too far. Either the tractor goes, or I go.

At first, the man who loved tractors was very happy, riding around in his tractor all day, and organising his collections by night. But after a while he started to feel lonely, and began to wonder if he might have made a terrible mistake, and if his single-minded pursuit of all things tractor might actually end up ruining his life. Reluctantly, he took his tractor back to the showroom for a tearful goodbye. He boxed up his models, and his books, and his paintings, and took every last one to the tractor-fanciers' market. And then he rang his wife, and told her that he was sorry, and that he was cured of his obsession. She was not entirely convinced that he was truly a changed man, but finally agreed to meet him at the restaurant they always used to go to together, back in the days when his love of tractors had seemed like nothing more than an endearing little quirk.

When we walk on to the place where the deer had

been, we come upon an explosion of feathers. Long primaries and tail feathers, and a mass of pure white wispy down from the breast, all grouped together in their place. It is like a deconstructed wood pigeon. A fresh kill, but with no trace of a body, nor even a drop of blood. It is hard to imagine that a single bird would have so many feathers. Somewhere, not far away, a female goshawk is feeding her young, being a dutiful parent. Out comes the camera for a forensic record; the mass of down is unsettlingly beautiful.

We emerge from the woods, and the tale of the man who loved tractors is brought to its inevitable end. The man and his wife were sitting at their favourite table, waiting for their dinner to arrive, when the chef burst out of the kitchen shouting: Help! Help! Fire! Fire! Great thick clouds of black smoke billowed into the room, and people began to cough and run around in circles flapping their arms. The man who loved tractors patted his wife reassuringly on the arm, and said: Don't worry, dear, I've got this. He stood up and puffed up his chest, and then with an immense intake of breath sucked up every last bit of smoke from the room before blasting it out of the window. Everybody cheered and applauded him for saving the day. His wife was flabbergasted. But how could you possibly do that? she asked. Simple, he said. I'm an ex-tractor fan.

I groan.

TEN

The Butterfly Effect

July 2019

It was back at the spring equinox that I saw my first
butterflies of the year. That was in Church Place
Inclosure, and I have returned to the same woods now
that the season should be at its peak. In the early twentieth
century, when butterfly collectors would flood the forest,
much to W. H. Hudson's disgruntlement, it was not to
the open forest that they were heading, but to the
enclosures where the butterflies' food plants had some
protection from livestock.

As I enter the woods I pass family parties and groups
out for a stroll. Along the ride are great clumps of
bramble in full bloom. They are alive with honey bees
and bumble bees, and with butterflies too; large skippers
and small skippers, and great numbers of ringlets.

Silver-washed fritillaries swoop in, swinging from bloom to bloom and barely settling for a moment. They are a glorious coppery-orange, stencilled with black. I just stand there and watch the vibrant, busy life all around me. It strikes me how seldom I have come across people out for a walk on their own in all my visits to the forest. The only solo visitors I have come across are occasional joggers or mountain bikers, who are not actually walkers, and occasional dog-walkers, who are not really alone. But here, up ahead, I can see a solitary man like me, similarly hovering around a clump of brambles, in rapt attention. He notices me and comes over. He asks if I have seen any white admirals yet, and I say no, not yet. Wait until the sun comes out, he says. There is a little cloud over the sun. And as soon as the sun breaks out, and a ray of sunshine hits the brambles, a white admiral comes sailing down from the trees and circles around me, brushing against my arm.

When Colin Tubbs wrote *The New Forest: A Natural History* back in the eighties, he feared for the future of the New Forest's butterflies, some of which had already become extinct locally. These two species, the silver-washed fritillary and the white admiral, had once been abundant, but were then barely hanging on. At that time, the enclosures were mostly open to livestock, either by intent or by reason of their fencing having fallen into disrepair, and were being grazed bare. Forest butterflies seemed to be in terminal decline. But they have been brought back from the brink by securing the enclosures again, and are flourishing once more. The life of the forest may be rooted in what seems like an almost unchanging landscape, but it can still be alarmingly fragile, and vulnerable to what may at first seem to be only cosmetic changes. Small choices can have major unforeseen consequences. The butterfly effect, only with the butterflies as the effect rather than the cause.

The butterfly man, whose name is Milan, is here trying to take some macro photographs. He shows me some; they look very professional. He teaches me, using his photographs, how to distinguish a male silver-washed from a female. I ask him if he has a blog where he posts his pictures, and he says no, that he has never quite got around to it, they are all just sitting in a file on his computer at home.

He asks if I have been to Standing Hat. Ah, I say, the pearl-bordered fritillary. I was there a little early in the season, and saw just one. You should have gone back a couple of weeks later, he says, it was the best year yet. While he was there watching them he met the man whose job it was to manage the rides, purely for the benefit of this one species, replicating the coppices where they once thrived. I admit that I am no great expert when it comes to butterflies, that I am still learning. In fact, though I am not too bad on birds and mammals, I am not really an expert on anything. More of a generalist than a specialist, I know a little about everything and a lot about nothing. I tell him I write books on nature and travel. So, he asks, will there be a book coming out set in the New Forest? Maybe, I say, in a year or two, these things take time. And I still need to find a publisher for it. But if it does come out, I'll put you in it.

We walk on together, off the main track and onto a narrow grassy ride that sees less foot traffic. We follow the sun, like the butterflies. There are clumps of bramble on both sides of the ride, but all the life is on the sunny side. I ask him if he has seen the valezina, something I would love to see. The valezina is a rare colour variant of the silver-washed fritillary, found only in the female, and it is strikingly different; much darker, and rather than a glorious orange it is a beautiful mossy teal colour. The early lepidopterist F. W. Frohawk, who wrote and illustrated the classic British butterfly books of the early twentieth century, and is still widely considered the greatest ever painter of butterflies, was so smitten by this rarity that he had his honeymoon here in the New Forest in order to, I suppose, mix pleasure with pleasure. I hope Mrs Frohawk was a fellow enthusiast; they would go on to name their daughter Valezina. That really is taking your work home with you. Milan tells me that although the forest is well known for sightings of this variety, they seem to have become much less frequent over the years; although he has seen them recently elsewhere in Hampshire, it is a decade since he last saw one in the forest itself.

The sunlit bank of bramble blossom we are standing beside is throbbing with life. There is even a damselfly resting on the topmost bloom. Many of the family are hard to tell apart, but this one is utterly distinctive. It has a metallic blue-green body and gingery wings. This is the beautiful demoiselle, a female, one of the very few species with coloured wings. The dragonflies and damselflies are not nectar-feeders – they are predators, one and all – and she is here in stealth mode, pretending to be harmless. She suddenly leaps up from her perch, almost too fast to see, and snatches successfully at a passing fly.

A white admiral comes winging in to join us. A female, Milan tells me, though I have no idea how he can tell with such ease. She immediately proves him right, however, for she flies through the tangle of brambles to the unnoticed vines of a honeysuckle coiling around a sapling behind, and begins to lay her eggs, one by one. While many butterflies may use a small range of food plants, the caterpillars of the white admiral live on honeysuckle and nothing else.

It is soon time for us to part ways; we were, after all, heading in opposite directions when we met. But just before I turn to leave, I have a thought. I get out my map, and ask Milan if he happens to know the whereabouts of a colony of the wild gladiolus. The gladiolus or sword-lily, a member of the iris family, is perhaps the most celebrated of all the forest's wild flowers; because it is startlingly beautiful with its fan of magenta flowers, because it is found nowhere else in Britain, because it lives in just a limited number of small colonies, and because it is notoriously hard to find. I could search for weeks without having any luck. He points a finger at a precise spot. Here, he says, but give it a week or two, they won't be quite ready yet. For good measure, he indicates where to find the coral necklace, another local speciality, found only in a couple of other locations in the whole of Britain.

We shake hands, and just as I am beginning to walk off, I notice a roe buck with a mouthful of grass, watching us curiously from no distance away at all. I indicate it to Milan, and the last I see of him he is stalking slowly towards the deer, camera in hand.

I walk off through the woods, with the butterflies dancing all around me. When I pass through the gate that leads me back onto open ground, I follow a grassy track along the edge of the trees. Away in another wood across the track, I can hear foresters at work, and there are signs advising against entry. Every little pool, even down to the size of a puddle, seems to be guarded by a single male chaser, circling watchfully, ready to fight, as if to say: This may not seem like much, but it is all mine. Everywhere there are painted lady butterflies, big and boldly patterned; I have never seen so many. This is a butterfly that migrates every year from North Africa into Europe. It seems incredible enough that small birds can make it all the way here from Africa; for fragile insects to do the same seems extraordinary. The ones I am seeing will never make the return trip. They will breed here and die here, and it is a new generation that will turn to the south when the weather cools. Most years their numbers remain relatively modest, but every decade or so when conditions in Morocco are just right, there will be a mass irruption, and great clouds of them will arrive on our shores. These are the very first I have seen this year, and they are everywhere, newly flown in from across the Channel. It is a painted lady year.

As I head out onto the heath, tiny silver-studded blues rise from my footfalls and spin in little circles around me. There seem to be far more males than females, or perhaps the females are just less active or less noticeable; they are duller, brown with orange spots rather than the brilliant blue of the males. These are the butterflies that I first saw on my last visit with my daughters, but now there are many more of them. They are like the little jewels of the heath. They spend much of their time settled on the heather, but my passing is enough to send them into a brief flurry of activity. The further out onto the heath I go, and the taller the heather, the more there seem to be; it is incredible to think that such a relatively scarce species could be so locally abundant when the conditions are just right. Finally, in the very middle of the heath, there is a band of heather that is almost waist height, and as I pass through it, hundreds upon hundreds of them, maybe thousands, all rise at once. They whirl around me, rising above my head, like a blue tornado sparkling in the sunshine. Never in all my travels have I seen so many butterflies all in one place, and I stop, amazed. I spread out my arms, reaching my hands into the swirl of intense blue life. It is like colour in motion, colour brought to life. A rhapsody in blue. Sometimes, just sometimes, if you are very lucky, nature will give you an unforgettable moment such as this, a moment that makes you feel that this is what life is all about.

When I get home, hours later, I go straight to my bookshelf. Something has snagged in my mind. I don't collect books; most I just read and pass on. I only keep those that I know I shall want to return to. Sometimes after re-reading a book, I will feel that its work is now done, and I shall pass that on too. There are fewer than a hundred books remaining, from a lifetime of reading. I reach for a collection by Matsuo Bashō, the seventeenth-century Japanese Zen poet, and flick through until I find what I am looking for:

> To talk casually
> About an iris flower
> Is one of the pleasures
> Of the wandering journey.

ELEVEN

A Fine Balance

July 2019

Between the woods and the heath is a dense band of fully grown bracken, acre upon acre of it. This could be harder than I thought, I consider to myself. How am I going to find them in all of this? The wild gladiolus survives by flowering beneath the canopy of the bracken. If it tried to grow anywhere else it would be eaten by the ponies, but bracken is distasteful to livestock and so the animals largely stay away from it. This does result in the flowers being rendered effectively invisible, however. You could be a foot away from one and still not see it. It is so well hidden that it escaped unnoticed until relatively recently. The trick, apparently, is to get right down and lie beneath the fronds so you can see a little way through the stalks.

I wade into the bracken and lie down. Right in front of me is my first gladiolus, in all its delicate beauty. It is not the most perfect specimen – its topmost flowers are still in bud, and the three flowers that are in full bloom have withered a little. But they live in colonies – there will surely be better examples nearby. I walk a few paces, then throw myself down, a few more paces, then down again. I wonder what I must look like to an unnoticed observer, yet am prepared to appear foolish if it's in a good cause. But my confidence in finding more is mistaken; no matter how much I scour the beds of bracken, it seems that a single slightly second-rate gladiolus will be my lot. It is as if they are sending me a message: Okay, you've found what you were looking for, now stop being greedy and leave us alone. And so I do, having learned my lesson. To be satisfied with my lot, and not always demand more, for that never ends; it is the path to perpetual dissatisfaction.

Leaving them in peace, I head off to search for the coral necklace, *Illecebrum verticillatum*. The coral necklace has very demanding habitat requirements, and is only found in numbers here and on Bodmin Moor in Cornwall. It needs ground that is inundated with water in winter but dries out in the summer. Its seeds are so fragile that they cannot compete with other plants, and so it grows principally on trails that have otherwise been trampled almost bare by livestock. Using the guidance I have been given, I find several clumps of it in quick succession. It is not a gaudy, glamorous plant like the gladiolus; it would be easy to pass it by without a second glance. But look closely and it has its own subtle beauty. Its long prostrate stems trail along the ground, bright red and encircled by rings of the tiniest white flowers. Up close and personal it is exquisite. Its jumble of coiled stems really does make it look like a cast-off necklace.

In similar spots, I have found two species of sundew; the round-leaved and the oblong-leaved. There is a third species too, the great sundew, but that lives right out in the mires where I would have to wade to be in with a chance of finding it. They are extraordinary-looking things, with brilliant red leaves covered in spines, and at the end of each spine a sticky droplet. I recall being fascinated by them as a child, as I am sure are many children, and some adults too; Charles Darwin wrote an entire book about them, experimenting obsessively with their dietary preferences. Plants that eat animals; they seem like a reversal of the natural order of things. And on the cracked banks of a shrunken Hatchet Pond, I found what looked like a fresh flush of grass, until I looked closer. The colour seemed somehow wrong, and instead of emerging sheath-like from the ground the blades unfurled from tiny fiddleheads. This was pillwort, *Pilularia globulifera*, a very scarce fern that grows to look like grass. It is found at a few sites in the UK, but is under threat and is in decline over the whole of Europe. If I had not been paying close attention, I would have missed it entirely, as I am sure most passers-by must. It looked like the lawn of an alien planet. It seems remarkable that such an arcane habitat – nutrient-poor soil, seasonally inundated, and trampled by livestock – should have developed its own array of frankly bizarre species, an ecology all its own.

Out on a heathland pool, blue damselflies are thronging, in constant motion. And then they all suddenly melt away. I soon see why, for an emperor has arrived. The emperor dragonfly, with its apple-green thorax and eyes, is huge in comparison. It is the apex predator of the family, with a diet that consists almost entirely of its relatives. In the past I have paid little mind to the dragonflies, but the more I see of them, the more fascinating I am beginning to find them. As with most things, I suppose. They all have their own very particular life cycles and habitat preferences. Two streams that look near-identical to me can have distinct ecologies that are invisible to the eye, and can support a wholly different range of species. The world is far more subtle and complex than it appears at first sight.

I pass off the heath and through wood pasture to the enclosures. While much of the forest is a scatter of woodland amongst heathland, in the heart of the forest is a great tract of woods. If you picked your route you could walk for miles, and for hours, without breaking cover. It is still and silent in here. There seem to be fewer butterflies about than on my last visit. Perhaps the season has passed its peak, or perhaps it is just that there is a little cloud cover today, and the butterflies are at their liveliest in bright sunshine. And then a pair of silver-washed fritillaries come dancing down the ride towards me, spiralling around each other in a double helix. As they pass me by, I see that one of them is decidedly darker than the other. I look closer; it is a valezina. I can scarcely believe that one has come to me when I had stopped hoping. I follow them down the ride, watching the dance of life, letting them lead me on, but they gradually pull away from me and disappear into the depths of the wood. They are strong fliers. In an ideal world, they would settle for a moment, so that I could get a protracted view, perhaps even get out my phone for a photo, but it is not to be. I have to remember the lesson of the gladiolus. We cannot make demands of nature, and should be thankful for every fleeting moment of grace that it affords us, for it exists for itself alone, not for our enjoyment.

Dragonflies propel themselves along the rides. They look somewhat similar to the emperor, but a little smaller. This is the southern hawker, a species that spends much of its time away from water. They patrol their territories in the forest clearings, beating the bounds. Ahead of me on the ride I come upon a little group of fallow deer; a doe, two yearlings and a fawn, my first fawn of the season. It is very young still, high-stepping and knock-kneed, and alarmingly cute for an animal that is seen in some quarters as a pest. I stop in my tracks so that they can drift away into the undergrowth without being panicked by my presence.

I circle out of the enclosures and back through a gate into the pasture woods. Because I am arriving on each visit by train, my walks tend to be either in great circles that take me back to where I came from, or dog-legs that take me from one station to another. Because the railway line skirts the east and south of the forest, this is where I have been concentrating my visits. I feel like I have been neglecting the north and west of the forest, where the landscape is markedly different. I am going to have to find a way to remedy this, for it was the north and west of the forest that I visited most in my childhood, and that is where so many of my memories reside.

Coming to a little wooden bridge over a fine stream, I decide that this is a good place for a pause in my walk. Walking in most of the plantations, I feel that I could be anywhere, but the wood pastures are utterly distinctive; you know you could only be in the New Forest. They feel ancient, timeless. The stream is humming with damsel-flies, dozens of them. These are the beautiful demoiselle, most of them males. I watch as one settles on a frond of bracken that overhangs the stream in a sunny spot. Its wings are a glorious metallic blue, and the sight makes me inexplicably happy. When you love nature it does not take much to bring you joy: a passing butterfly, an orchid in bloom, or in this case the shining wings of a damselfly as it grooms itself on the tip of a fern. I recognise that I am easily pleased. It is my own particular pathology, I think; my resting state, alone in a room doing nothing, is one of fundamental contentment. It does not take much to make me happy, and an awful lot to make me sad. If I sometimes feel the urge to explore the darker side of life, or to dwell on the melancholic, it is because I know that I am only paying a visit from a place of safety. It is said that we all have our own default mood; that a lottery winner will be temporarily ecstatic, but before long will revert back to being just as happy as she was before; no more, no less. But there are a few things that can lift your mood in the longer term; one of them is altruism, doing things for the benefit of others, and another is spending time out in nature.

I sit on the rail of the bridge with my feet dangling and look upstream to where the waters wind their way out of the woods, banks overhung with ferns. I unwrap half my sandwich and put the other half on the rail beside me. There is a plop as I accidentally nudge the sandwich

beside me so it falls midstream, and I laugh at my clum-
siness. I get down off the bridge and lie on the grassy
bank, stretching out to try to retrieve it. It is still wrapped
and I don't want to leave any litter. Not quite able to reach
it, I stretch out a little further, and a little further. Then I
think to myself: You're going to fall in the water, aren't
you? I get up to look for a suitable stick to go sandwich
fishing, and wait while my errant lunch floats slowly
beneath the bridge. You are a ridiculous person, I think
to myself. I have witnesses too, of sorts. A small group of
nearby ponies come cantering over as if to see what I am
up to. Being semi-wild, the ponies mostly keep their
distance and largely ignore passers-by, apart from a few
that have taken to hanging around the car parks like
gangs of unruly teenagers, leading to signs urging people
not to pet them or feed them treats, and to the provision
of pony-proof litter bins. The leader of this group, a bay
mare, seems very self-confident, though. She nuzzles
me, then sniffs at the soggy sandwich at my feet, before
snorting and nudging it back to me.

The ponies drink at the stream and then wander off,
their curiosity satisfied. I sit on the grass bank in dappled
oak-light, and watch the damselflies as they whirr and

skirmish over the clouded ruddy waters, and soak up the vitality of the living forest that seems to throb with an energy all its own. There is a growing understanding of just how sophisticated woodland ecology can be; of how the roots of trees may be interconnected through fungal hyphae, of how they may share nutrients with one another, of how they may communicate with one another by chemical means to warn that they are being attacked by browsers or caterpillars, for instance. Of how an entire woodland may almost function as an interwoven superorganism rather than an assemblage of competing individuals. The fact that plants may have greater sentience than has been assumed does not necessarily imply that they have anything we humans would recognise as a consciousness, however. We tend to look at the evolution of species over time as being an isolated phenomenon, the gradual improvement of a creature's fitness. But, of course, it is not like that at all. Everything affects everything else; we are all on this journey together. Ecosystems evolve, just as surely as do species. As I sit by my stream-side I try to imagine what this spot might have looked like millennia ago, but it is beyond me. The stream might possibly have already been here, but other than that it would have looked different, sounded different, smelt different, and above all had its own character, its own atmosphere; one that I can only guess at.

Evolution follows the path of possibility, nothing more, nothing less; an endless experiment with no purpose, no goal, not even a direction. There is no real hierarchy in evolution either. So far as we can tell, life began just once, and from there exploded into a vast multiplicity of forms and expressions of possibility. The slug at our feet, and the blade of grass it is munching on, have both been evolving for just the same length of time that we have. And there is nothing to stop evolution leading to an organism that has the capacity to bring all life to an end. There is no judgement here; sometimes the solutions evolution comes up with may be pretty, and sometimes . . . not so much. Something close to half of the animal species on earth are parasites. We have come to understand just how connected and inter-dependent communities of plants and animals may be. But I do not think we are doing these living communities any favours by trying to portray their essence as being more like our own than it really is; surely a big part of the wonder of nature is its sheer otherness. Perhaps the portrayal of nature as intrinsically benevolent is a balancing of the scales, from when it was perceived as an enemy to be subdued, something of which we were not a part, and evolution was portrayed as an arms race, and to the winner the spoils. We may be inclined to think of extinct creatures as having failed, and yet many lost species will not have disappeared through a failure to adapt, but through their success, gradually evolving new species and still remaining part of the unbroken chain. And many of them may have survived for a much longer time on earth than we are ever likely to. We are new kids on the block; as things stand we are not even the longest surviving species of human. *Homo neanderthalensis* was around on earth for significantly longer than *Homo sapiens* has managed to be, at least up until now, and the signs are not looking that great for us to be around for all that much longer. If the whole history of the earth is ever to be written, I doubt we will take up much of it; we will be there as a flash in the pan, a brief moment of trouble, like a meteorite strike.

We should be able to value nature for itself, without passing moral judgement. It is possible to sit in the shade of a tree and appreciate it for what it is without feeling the need to attribute to it an imagined kindliness that is nothing more than a projection of our own desires. By all means hug a tree if it makes you feel good; the tree won't mind at all, but don't kid yourself that it is hugging you back. It is a leap of the imagination to conceive of what it might feel like to be another person, let alone another animal or a plant. Sometimes I feel that I barely understand what it means to be me. Perhaps I have this all wrong, perhaps there are other ways of seeing, and I am just handicapped by the limitations of my own perspective. Do other people see what I see when they walk through the woods? The answer, I think, is not really, or not entirely. We may all begin at the same starting line, but we then grow to face the world through a tangled web of culture and memory, and, indeed, of imagination. Perhaps, as I sit among the woods, the trees really are whispering to me, and I simply don't have the capacity to hear them. Perhaps the trees are calling: Hug me, hug me, and I am just stubbornly turning my back on them. But I doubt it, and there is no way that I could ever know, and I am content not to.

It is possible, I hope, to simply be awestruck by the

immense variety of life, its beauty, its vitality, its complexity. The lovely wood in which I find myself is a product of neither unbridled competition, nor of cooperation, alone, but rather the place where these two forces meet; creativity and destruction, hand in hand. Evolution leads to an exquisite balance of forms, in a state of constant fluctuation, shifting moment by moment in infinitesimal changes, which, given enough time, will transform the place entirely. The sophistication of all this is almost beyond comprehension. It is a wonder.

It is, of course, also possible for this balance to be disrupted. Rats will arrive on an island that has no ground predators and the local ecology may be devastated. We see the problems caused by invasive plants, such as rhododendrons, Japanese knotweed or Himalayan balsam. In their native environment, alongside a network of life that has evolved with them, they create no problems at all – they are a part of the balance. Some of our own native plants, which fit in nicely here, can be a huge problem elsewhere. The purple loosestrife, which I have seen growing in reed beds here in the forest, is a great source of food for nectar-feeders, and is attractive enough to be planted in gardens. In North America, where it was taken as a decorative plant, its population has exploded, and it is strangling vast areas of their native wetlands. And the European gorse, so much an integral part of this landscape, this ecosystem, has now become the most destructive invasive plant in New Zealand.

Humans are an invasive species too. As we spread our way around the globe over the course of some fifty thousand years, native megafauna largely disappeared from the earth, continent by continent, island by island, almost immediately upon our arrival. The megafauna, outsized animals that were long-lived and reproduced slowly, and suffered from low rates of predation of mostly just their weakest members, were not equipped to deal with the arrival of what was basically a super-predator. They did not need to be actively wiped out; the loss of a small number of them was enough to shift the balance between life and death, and nudge them into a rapid spiral of decline. The only continent on earth that still has a substantial relic population of megafauna is Africa, where they evolved alongside us, where we spent most of our history as part of the native ecology. We have the capacity to effect change that is too fast for evolution to keep up with.

The air, the water, the energy of the sun, the land itself, are all one great commons; a commons not just for people but a shared resource for life itself. We have turned ourselves into landlords, parcelled the world up among ourselves as enclosures, turned it into our own private fiefdom. Evolution has no choice in what it does, but we do, as a species, if not always as individuals. Unless we can learn to see ourselves not as masters of the world, but simply as the personification of a life that has expanded to include millions of different species, then the future does not look bright. We have set the world off balance; it is surely up to us to put it right.

TWELVE

Fern Owl and Fuzzacker

August 2019

The path leads up the hillside before me and I begin to make my way up onto the ridge. The bus had dropped me in Fordingbridge, and I had crossed the old bridge over the River Avon and walked a couple of miles along narrow lanes to make it back to the forest. The landscape here in the north-west of the forest is quite distinctively different. Further south, the land rolls gently, while here it reaches its greatest heights in a series of high gravel ridges that run west to east. It is hardly what you would call rugged, but still looks a little wilder and less bucolic. The trail runs along the summit of Hampton Ridge, with long views north and south, big sky views. And the heath in every direction is lit up with a mauve wash. While the pinks and purples of the bell heather and the cross-leaved heath have been in bloom for some time, now they have been joined by the true heather, the ling. The purple haze of the moors in August. The spectacle is not quite as it should be, however. Heat stress, drought, climate change; the heather is failing. On many plants, the buds have failed to bloom, and they have browned and shrivelled. A result of last year's droughts, followed by a mild winter that has enabled pests to survive. And this year, while there have been wet spells, they have been interspersed with heatwaves that have crested higher than ever before.

It is a long, long time since I was last in this part of the forest. When they divorced, my parents each took custody of a handful of the belongings left behind by my brother and myself. In another childhood diary that I have recently acquired from my mother, I can see that I first came here two days after my twelfth birthday. My diary says that, on that visit, I came upon a pair of Dartford warblers. It was on the same day that I had already been watching red-backed shrikes a little further north. That was a very good day. Both of these birds have eluded me ever since, at least here in Britain. The red-backed shrike is no longer to be seen, but the warbler could well be. It is a bird I would love to see once again, after all these years.

The Dartford warbler is a rare, specialised bird of the lowland heaths; so particular in its requirements that it can live nowhere else, so it is utterly dependent on a vanishing habitat. It nests in the heather, and feeds almost exclusively in the gorse brakes. Here in the New Forest, in the neighbouring Dorset heaths, what is left of the Surrey heaths and a handful of other fragmentary heathlands, and that is it. It got its name because the original specimens from which the species was first identified were shot long ago at Bexleyheath, near Dartford in Kent. But about two centuries ago, the area got its own Enclosure Act. It is a long time since there was last a heath in Bexleyheath, and a long time since there was a Dartford warbler in Dartford. It is such a characteristic feature of the life of the forest that it has acquired its own local name – the fuzzacker. There is a theme developing here, though I have no idea what the 'acker' might be. Perhaps it is meant to represent its call.

I have been searching for this secretive little bird all year long, but it has remained resolutely hidden. One visit after another, I have never knowingly passed a gorse brake without feeling compelled to scour it for the elusive fuzzacker, but to no avail. So here I am, back in the very area where I saw it all those decades ago; the one time I met with success. Sometimes you have to go back to move forwards. High on the summit of the ridge, close to where I remember seeing the birds all those years ago, I come upon a large area of regenerating gorse that looks just the right habitat. I slip between two bushes and enter what looks like a maze: clumps of gorse, the spaces between them like prickly tunnels, interspersed with sudden clearings filled with masses of high-growing heather of all types and colours, less heavily grazed up here. And it takes me just a minute to find a pair of the warblers. They are tiny birds, with extravagantly long tails. Unlike the vast majority of warblers, which come in shades of pastel, these are distinctively dark in appearance. They have bright red eyes, their upper parts are a deep bluish-grey, almost purple, and their breasts are a dull red. They look like little plums; plums on a stick.

In the next gorse-brake I investigate, I find another pair, in the following one a single bird, and so on. Everywhere I look, I seem to find them. An embarrassment of fuzzackers. It is a relief to think they are apparently doing so well; my inability to locate them earlier in the year had left me concerned for their welfare. This is a bird prone to extreme fluctuations in its population. Unlike the vast majority of warblers, which migrate every winter to warmer climes, the Dartford warbler goes nowhere, and being reliant on invertebrate prey, tiny insects and spiders that it finds amongst the undergrowth, it is very susceptible to prolonged cold snaps in winter. During the famously severe winter of 1962–63 it is believed that as few as six pairs survived, and it took many years for the population to recover. I come upon a family of wheatears too. These are a common sight in the uplands of the north and the west, but, here in the deep south, only a few pairs stay to breed. You are much more likely to see them on passage, during the spring and autumn migration; I remember watching out for them on the hill where I grew up, for they would often be the very first bird to arrive to our shores, a harbinger of spring. A day or so later they would all be gone; off to the high hills of northern England, or Scotland or Wales, where I had never been.

It is peaceful up here on the ridge, with expansive views over heaths that don't even seem to contain any livestock, let alone people. But it was not always so. During wartime, the whole area was taken over by the RAF, and was used as the Ashley Walk bombing range. The bouncing bomb, of *Dam Busters* renown, was first tested here, in dry runs before being tried out over water. Also tested here was the Grand Slam, at ten thousand kilos the largest bomb ever to fall on British soil. Most of the damage has been restored, but traces still remain, eighty years on, and the heath is pocked with hidden craters. As I walk along the ridge, I am surprised to see a giant arrow half-hidden in the gorse and the heather. It is a hundred feet long and made of concrete, embedded in the ground trailside and pointed right at me. A directional marker for passing bombers. Bombs away. It makes me feel momentarily self-conscious, as if I've been caught out and the finger of God is holding me to account. Later, I come upon a little brick shelter, three-sided like some bus shelters or bird hides, and looking completely out of place, as if left here by accident. It has concrete windows with long horizontal slots not more than an inch high that look out across the expanse of Ashley Walk. An observation post. A good place to sleep if it was raining, I think to myself. It is the habit of a lifetime, from the years spent hitching round the world with nothing but a sleeping bag, to ask myself this question. A reflex, on every walk I take: Where would I sleep, if I had to? Here are some of the places I have spent the night when caught out by rain: under countless bridges; in innumerable ruins and building sites; in caves; in bandstands; in hollow trees; under a lifeguard's hut; in an empty tollbooth; in a disused pigsty; in a Mayan tomb.

While I was up on the high ridge, there was little sign of any livestock, but as soon as I begin to drop downhill, the ponies and cattle reappear. There is even a little herd of deer, one of them entirely black in colour, with a couple of fawns folded up at their feet. I walk on to Cooper's Hill, and wonder idly if there is a possible family connection. My mother was born a Cooper. My grandfather was born nearby, and the Coopers were quite a tribe; I don't doubt that I still have distant relatives out on the fringes of the forest. I never met my grandfather; he died before I was born. My mother has often said how she wished we could have known each other. We would have got on, she is convinced; he loved nature, knew his birds.

I acknowledge that the deep connection I feel with this landscape stems from the time I spent here as a child. It is tempting, too, to feel that the fact that I have family roots here gives me an extra sense of belonging. But is it really possible to have a sense of connection that is passed on down the generations other than by culture and the telling of stories? An ancestral homeland that is our true place on earth, even if we have never set foot there? The kind of localism that makes us feel a passionate connection to a particular place on earth can be a positive thing; it can make us fight for our corner and preserve it for future generations. But it is not a big step from believing that family history can tie you to one small corner of the world to believing that you can only really belong in a place if you have deep roots there. The land of my forefathers. And then the next step is that you claim rights above others. Yet wherever we are on earth, we are immigrants; it is just a matter of when. Whoever we are, we can be sure that our ancestors at some point arrived here from somewhere else. The study of ancestry is intriguing to many, it can give us a sense of identity, of our place in the scheme of things. It is no bad thing to honour our ancestors, and remember their struggles, but ultimately it does not change anything about us; it just becomes a story that we tell ourselves about where we like to think that we belong. As I wander these trails through heath and wood, I find it intriguing to imagine that I may be following in the footsteps of my ancestors, but must remind myself that this gives me no special relationship with this place, and no intrinsic insight; I must earn that by myself, one step at a time.

The path leads down into woods; an old enclosure that is open now, a great mix of full-grown pine and oak and beech. At the very edge of the woods is a huge flock of willow warblers. They fly out from the trees and hover like hummingbirds as they snatch at passing insects. There are more warblers in this one flock than I have seen the entire year. My no longer being able to hear their song has not helped me to spot them. I head deep into the woods; it is evening now and I have them all to myself. Any other walkers have headed home but I am going to spend the night in the forest. I know that wild camping is not actually permitted here, but if I have no tent and lie down under a tree for the night, leaving no trace, can I really be said to have been camping? I come to a footbridge over the Latchmore Brook, but the stream has run dry, now just a series of disconnected muddy pools. There is no flow. The ride is crossed by a well-worn badger trail. The sett must be near, I think. I could follow the trail back to their home, position myself downwind, and watch as they emerge for the night. But I have other plans.

To be alone in the woods at night is sometimes thought to be intimidating. We may flinch at the cracking of a twig in the shadows, worry that we are being watched by unseen eyes. But for whatever reason I never feel like that; I find the forest by night to be comforting. The sun will be setting soon, and I need to find my spot before it gets dark. My intention is not to stay in the darkest depths of the wood, but to position myself at its edge, the interface where one habitat meets another, where I hope there will be more to be seen. Where the wood meets the heath there is a fine scattering of Scots pines that have self-seeded and are slowly creeping out into the heather. I find a perfect spot; almost level and nestled between a group of five trees that have grown close together. There is no obvious route between the trees, and my biggest worry is of getting trampled by cattle as they bumble about in the dark. I lay out my sleeping bag; from here I have a perfect view into the woods, out onto the heath, and up to a circle of sky framed by branches.

My sleeping spot falls into shadow, and then a dark band slowly creeps up the trunks of the trees as the sun sinks in the sky. I am on the eastern flank of Cooper's Hill, so will not be able to see the sun setting from here. I decide to stroll up the hillside for a longer view. As I climb, I find that I have to circumnavigate a pair of bomb craters, almost hidden now amongst the heather; a trap for the unwary. In a band of gorse, I get a final perfect view of a fuzzacker skipping from bush to bush. My best view of the day as well as my last. I lost count at some point earlier on, but it must be well over ten I've seen. Through the thick heather ahead of me, I see what looks like a pair of sticks bouncing along the ridge line, silhouetted against the reddening sky. Where there is a break in the heather, a roe buck turns to look at me almost indifferently, a handsome fellow with his big black nose and small fine antlers. As the sun approaches the horizon, it passes behind a distant bank of low cloud and is lost to view. I shall not get the full sunset effect after all. Perhaps it is a good thing; I need to get back down the hill while it is still light enough to see. I don't want to stumble into a crater in the dark.

I lie down on my back beneath the pine trees and wait. The ground is a soft enough mix of pine needles and grass, the weather is still and dry and mild, and there seem to be no biting insects to trouble me. I could not have asked for better conditions for a night out under the stars. I don't have long to wait; almost immediately what I'd hoped to see appears right above my head at treetop height. Long sharp wings and a long, long tail, twisting and turning, spinning in circles, darting from side to side with astonishing grace, chasing moths. It is an almost mythical creature; the nightjar, the fern owl, the goatsucker, the nighthawk. I am inordinately pleased, aware that I have left it late in the season to look for one. In a week or two they will all be gone. And I have had no advice on where exactly to look for one; I have chosen this spot by intuition alone. It just felt right. And it is such a great view, for the light is barely beginning to fade, and the bird is so close, as if it has come to watch over me. It is unusual for a nightjar to put in an appearance until half an hour after sunset. I check the time; it is the precise minute of sunset.

These birds are more often heard than seen. They have an alien song, a mechanical churring that rises and falls, that is far-carrying and almost impossible to locate. Although personally I can never place any sound, as I only have one functioning ear. I never had the good fortune to see a nightjar here as a child, though I have seen them since, most recently when I was in Africa. I was hitch-hiking at night along a dirt road in the Kalahari Desert in Botswana, and they were swooping in and out of the darkness as they hoovered up the moths drawn to the beam of the car headlights. There are two or three other species of nightjar in Africa, but the ones I saw could well have been our own European variety, for they overwinter in sub-Saharan Africa.

Though I didn't get to see one as a child, I am nonetheless reminded of one night in the forest when I was twelve. I left my campsite at dusk, and climbed into a high seat – a wooden platform in the trees used for culling deer – that overlooked a little clearing, and watched a woodcock roding. It circled the clearing over and over with its strange moth-like flight, calling repeatedly, a frog-like croak followed by a high-pitched chirrup. I watched until the light failed, and the roe deer began to slip out of the cover of the trees. All the crep-uscular birds – the birds of the half-light – have a strange mystique about them. Seeing them is like peering through a curtain, and gaining a glimpse of an unseen world that runs in parallel to our own.

There are species of nightjar on every continent save for Antarctica, and they are one of the least known and most elusive of all families of birds. There are three species – from the Chinese desert, from the Congo basin, and from French Guiana – that are known from only a single specimen. And, notoriously, there is one species that is known from even less than a single specimen; one left wing, to be precise, which is all that could be salvaged from a roadkill bird found on the Nechisar Plain in central Ethiopia.

I hear no song. The bird I have been watching is a female, and the song is reserved for the male. It is light enough to see that she does not have the distinctive white wing patches of the male. I strain to hear if there is a more distant singing bird, but there is nothing. Perhaps it is too late in the season for song, or perhaps her mate has already left. After a while, she swoops elegantly away over the trees and is lost to view. Such a perfect sighting of such an extraordinary creature; it makes me feel emotional, like falling in love. Whatever the future brings, I will always have this moment. As I said, I am easily pleased.

It seems that the moment is over, but five minutes later she is back again, right above my head, and this becomes a pattern for the next half-hour. Every five minutes, almost to the dot, she comes back. It is as if she is watching over me, examining this inexplicable intrusion into her terrain, or perhaps it is just that she has a regular circuit, like the roding woodcocks of long ago. Darkness begins to fall. There is the merest sliver of a crescent moon. The stars come out, one by one, and the bats begin to circle around me, unidentifiable in the darkness. Just as I am beginning to think it will soon be too dark to see the nightjar again, I hear a gentle call – *coo-ic, coo-ic* – not the song but the flight call. She's back. And here she is, a shadow dancing over me. I watch until I can see nothing, then close my eyes and fall asleep with a smile on my face.

THIRTEEN

Returns

August 2019

The bus drops me off in Burley. This being summer, and the holiday season, the village centre is thronging with visitors, and I head out quickly along lanes towards my destination. The lane I am following crosses a little bridge, and I pause for a moment dead centre. Is it possible to walk over a bridge without stopping in the middle, leaning on the rail, and looking down at the waters flowing below? Certainly not for me. And on this occasion, I am pleased that I have paused, for there is a flash of neon as a kingfisher passes under the bridge and jets off downstream. Always in such a hurry to be somewhere. They race through life, as well they must, for they live on the edge; few of them survive past their first breeding season, if they even make it that far. They live furiously.

My goal is to head to the site of my very first camping trip in the forest, back when I was eleven. I can still remember the exact location with startling clarity. It was the early seventies, the last year that wild camping was permitted here. The problem was not so much the camping itself, but the number of people who were driving vehicles out onto the heaths and churning up the ground, and therefore disturbing the wildlife. I am reflecting on why it is that I feel compelled to revisit my childhood turf, or why now, at any rate. When you are young, you have a forward momentum, your focus is on the future, on where you are heading, you barely take pause to look back. But in everybody's life comes a mid-point, when as much of your life is behind you as it is before you. You can, of course, never know quite when that point is. I like to hope that when I hit it, I was doing something exciting, rather than drinking beer in front of the TV, or shopping. Though you can never know the moment, there comes a time when you have to be realistic and acknowledge that it is behind you, in the past. Undoubtedly, having children changes your perspective too; you no longer see yourself as at the cutting edge, but as part of a continuum of life, and you become more reflective about who you are, and what made you that way.

I leave the roadside where the farmland that surrounds the village meets the forest, and head out onto the heaths in baking-hot sunshine. Far from the woods I come upon a fine heathland pool filled with blooming waterlilies. To reach it I have to jump across a series of boggy drains; to call them streams would be an exaggeration. I can only reach the pool because there has been so little rain; I imagine that for most of the year the pool would be unattainable without some serious boggy wading. An emperor dragonfly is circling the pool imperiously, and in one of the drains I spot a much smaller dragonfly, a keeled skimmer, hiding in the sphagnum moss, my first sighting of one. I get out my notebook and add it with pleasure to my tally, for it has such a satisfying name. I shall probably not see many more species this year – the season will soon be coming to an end. Nonetheless, I have seen fourteen varieties of dragonflies and damsel-flies altogether, precisely half of the number of species in the forest, and those without making any effort to track them down, so I am content. I sit by the pool and soak in the atmosphere. In the mud at the water's edge I spot a single abandoned sandal. I'll bet there is a story there.

I leave the heath and pass through a plantation on my way to Berry Wood. Along the sides of the ride I spot my first mushrooms of the year, little clusters of golden chanterelles. I am tempted to harvest them, using the Potawatomi model – take half, leave half – but it is probably better just to leave them be. In a month or two the forest will be thick with mushrooms and toadstools. I shall try to spot the generous handful that I can recognise. There are supposedly some three thousand species of fungi in the forest – far too many for me to identify more than a small proportion – with new species being found all the time. Hidden beneath our feet for most of the year, their great flowering each autumn is another sign of the richness and longevity of the forest.

Berry Wood is just as I remember it from all those years ago; a superb example of pasture woodland. A mix of old oak and beech and holly, some of the finest I have seen anywhere, many with massive trunks and low crowns where they must have been pollarded hundreds of years ago. There are fallen trees everywhere, and many of those still standing have shed a bough or two. The trees are riddled with woodpecker holes. Mostly those of the great spotted woodpecker but also some much larger nesting holes of the green woodpecker. Green wood-peckers seem much less numerous than I remember them; I have only seen a couple all year. I stop to examine what is clearly a nesting hole, and a fairly freshly excavated one at that, about thirty feet up on a thick bough. If I had spotted it earlier in the season, I might have been able to watch them at the nest, but the young will have fledged by now.

At the edge of the wood where there has been a mass fall, scrub has grown up between the fallen branches, and the clearing that has been formed is sparkling with birds. When the breeding season ends and the birds abandon their territories, their even spread throughout the habitat that suits them breaks down, and they may gather together into roaming flocks that you can stumble upon almost anywhere. You can walk a long way seeing nothing and then suddenly come upon a great gathering of different species all drawn to the same spot. Here there are the inevitable fuzz-jacks aplenty, but there is also a family party of long-tailed tits twirling among the branches, and, in the scrub, groups of warblers and pipits and flycatchers, birds I have scarcely seen all year. From a treetop at the edge of the clearing, a buzzard is watching me, watching them.

The trail leads out of the woods and onto the heath where we set up our camp all those years ago. The heather appears to be in good health, and seems to have fared much better here than on some of the heaths I have visited. The horizon looks instantly familiar; the sweep of Berry Wood to one side of me, another small clump of trees here, the roll of the heath, a ridge line there, the flank of a more distant wood. I remember it all so precisely that I can triangulate myself within the landscape to get myself to the exact spot where I pitched my tent the last time I was here, all those years ago. Almost half a century ago; incredible. Where did the time go? Am I really the same person now that I was then? I sit amongst the heather. Great numbers of painted lady butterflies flutter from heather flower to heather flower. This must be a new generation, born here this summer. I can hear laughter echoing in the distance. Not human laughter, but green woodpecker laughter. I look about, but can't see it; I can't pinpoint where the sound is coming from. Instead I see a pair of black-and-white spotted woodpeckers just overhead, rising and falling in flight like they do, crossing the heath from wood to wood.

I don't know quite what I am doing here, what it is that has drawn me to come back and revisit the precise location of a childhood memory. I feel an intense sense of familiarity, and a glimpse of the continuity of life, of my life, but also a vague unease, a sense that something is missing. I think perhaps that I was unconsciously seeking something a little more: a flash of inspiration, a wave of self-awareness, a greater sense of my place in the great web of life. Illumination. I have form when it comes to going back.

A few years ago, I returned to the scene of that childhood fire, out of a sense of unfulfilled curiosity. When we moved away to the place that was to be home for the remainder of my childhood, we were not all that far away from our original house; only three or four miles. Often enough when we were out driving in the car we would pass the end of the lane, and my brother and I would ask if we could take a look at the old place. But my father would always have a reason not to, not today; we were on our way somewhere, or it was too late, or there was nothing to see anyway. And so we never did. And when I left home, I was either living far away, or in another country altogether, and my mind was far away too, so that returning to where I had grown up was the last thing on my mind. And then a few years ago it struck me that life had led me to as close as I had ever been to my home town, just a couple of hours away, and if not now, then when?

I took the train to Cosham, and then a local bus inland. The bus dropped me right at the end of the lane. It was a throbbingly hot and still summer's day. The lane was tarmacked now; back then it had still been gravel, and I walked down the middle of the road, as there was no traffic. In fact there didn't seem to be anyone about at all; no one in their gardens, no sign of life in any of the row of bungalows. Everything was completely still and silent, as if I had walked into a frozen moment. The houses looked smaller than I remembered them, and closer together. My perspective had changed; I was bigger now, of course. I walked past the spot where our house had once been; there were two houses on the old plot now, semi-detached. I walked on to the site of the place we had stayed that winter in extremis, but got no flash of recognition; I couldn't even be sure if it was the same house, or if it had been replaced. I didn't want to stop and stare, didn't want to seem to be acting suspiciously to any unseen observers, so I walked on to the end of the lane, and then turned and backtracked. Perhaps my father had been right all along, perhaps there really was nothing to see here. I stopped for one last look at the place where our house had once been, all those years ago. And then the lights went out.

During a total eclipse, as the shadow of the earth transits the face of the sun, there is a slow, almost imperceptible dimming of the light, but at the moment of totality, it is like a shutter snapping closed, and near-complete darkness falls almost instantaneously, at the speed of the turning of the earth. The suddenness of it takes your breath away. It was like that.

I had not moved an inch, I was still standing right there in the middle of the road, but in front of me was a burning building, with a cluster of agitated people at the door. Sirens wailed as the fire engines turned into the lane. Every one of my senses was fully engaged; I could smell acrid smoke, feel cold air on my skin, see the flicker of shadows, hear the mutter of many voices. If you have what I can only describe as a vision that is indistinguishable from the real world, you cannot help but question the solidity of the ground on which you stand.

The lights came on, and I was back. Not a thing had changed, but my heart lurched as if I had just stepped off a precipice. What the hell was that? It was not a memory, for my perspective had been different; I was an observer rather than a participant. I had just stood by and watched as my childhood self was carried out of the house, handed to a stranger, and bundled off down the road. Not a memory, then, but more, I suppose, a reconstruction. It felt more like time travel than memory. I shook my head and set off back to the bus stop. The mind is a strange thing. Reality is a strange thing. I think of myself as a grounded person, rooted to the here and now, a person of close attention, who looks intently at his surroundings and knows what he sees. Just occasionally along comes a reminder that perhaps my trusted way of seeing may not be the only way to look at the world.

I rouse myself from my resting place, deep in the buzzing, blooming heather of my childhood campsite, and set off across the heath. After a while I find myself in a field of blackjacks. By tradition, every winter a small portion of the furze growing on the heaths is burnt off, just a couple of per cent of it, presumably to prevent it taking over too much of the heathland, and to allow young heather to regenerate. The spiny leaves are all scorched away, but the jagged, blackened stalks remain, and these are known locally as blackjacks. Walking in the forest you come upon these small scorched patches of furze quite regularly. They are ugly, and walking through them can feel something like walking through a nightmare, but not knowing any better, I have to assume that this annual burn is an integral part of the management cycle of the forest, and is not just about freeing up a bit of extra space in order to squeeze in a few more livestock. It is quite possible that it is good environmental practice, but I have to admit that it still sits somewhat uncomfortably with me at a time when it sometimes feels that half the world is burning. While the other half is drowning.

FOURTEEN

The Dispossessed

September 2019

After the heavy rains of June, much of the summer has been hot and dry, often very hot and very dry, but when I arrive for the autumn equinox, the skies have opened, and there is torrential rain across much of the country, even floods. It is as though the usual rules no longer apply, and the normal fluctuations of the weather are being overwhelmed by the changing climate. Nothing is in moderation any more; when it is hot, it bakes, and when it rains, it pours. Perhaps it is time to stop being so cautious in our language, and to call it out for what it is: a climate catastrophe, in tandem with a mass extermination event. At ten in the morning, when the sun finally breaks through and I set off from Lyndhurst, it has been raining non-stop for eighteen hours. It is such a contrast to my last visit, not two weeks ago, when it still felt as if summer was at its peak.

I had travelled to Beaulieu Heath, a vast flat expanse of heathland in the south-east of the forest. In wartime, it had been used as an aerodrome, and although the runways are gone now, the road marking its periphery still persists, so the track around the heath is a broad roadway of crumbling concrete that forms a huge lozenge wrapped around the site of the former airfield. On the horizon I could see the far turrets of the Fawley oil refinery, like a distant threat. It is lucky that the prevailing wind blows the pollution away from the forest, rather than towards it.

I had come here in the faint hope of seeing a hobby before they all departed for Africa; this was the place where I last saw one in the forest, and I knew this would be my last chance. The hobby is an exquisite little falcon, incredibly graceful on the wing, that thrives in the forest. It is almost the only predator with the skills to catch swallows and martins and other masters of the air, though it mostly pursues dragonflies. It is quite a sight to see one snatch a dragonfly on the wing. But though I spent all day out on the heath, the skies remained stubbornly empty; empty of birds, empty of clouds. All I saw was a company of linnets in the furze and the scrub. I have been looking out for hobbies all summer long. I have been in the right places at the right times, but they have nonetheless eluded me. Perhaps it is a good thing that not every one of my hopes has been fulfilled; it leaves me with goals for the future.

I did, however, see something completely unexpected. My long walk to the heath took me through conifer plantations, and as I was skirting the edge of an area of recent clearcut, a little animal appeared on the forest track ahead of me, not much bigger than a fox. It was utterly unmistakable, with a wedge-shaped head close to the ground, longer back legs so that its rump was in the air: a muntjac. By far the most common deer in the forest is the long-ago introduced fallow, followed by the native roe. In the west of the forest is a herd of native red deer, and in the south-east a herd of the closely related sika deer. Attempts are made to keep these herds separate, for they are prone to interbreeding; many red deer populations in Scotland are thought to have been affected by cross-breeding. But of the five species of deer in the New Forest, the muntjac is by far the fewest in number.

It was first brought from China to Woburn Park in Bedfordshire early in the twentieth century and, following a series of escapes and deliberate releases, has slowly spread around the country; in some places it has become quite numerous, to the point of concern, but not here, at least not yet. They are few in number, shy and nocturnal, and live only in the remotest thickets. Seldom seen, they are not something you would ever look out for, and yet here was one wandering in a sunny clearing in broad daylight. An alien creature, for sure, and that is enough to enrage some people, but also a living being, and a beautiful one at that, just trying to get by like everything else. I am pleased to have spotted it.

My route from Lyndhurst takes me first across the golf course. There is no one at all out on the links, with the rain just having stopped. The course does not appear flooded, but the ground is sodden. Every footfall I make sends a spray of water circling out in all directions, and my shoes are soon soaked through. Ever the optimist, I have forgotten to bring my boots. Summer has turned to autumn since my last visit and everything looks quite different from just a week or two ago. The bracken has not yet collapsed, but has half-turned, so that much of it is a glorious coppery-orange in hue. The oaks are still in full leaf, but the beeches and birches are starting to deepen in colour too, and the first leaves are falling. The woods are stunning; I know this happens every year but it is easy to forget just how beautiful the season can be. When I first started these regular visits to the forest, it was in the depths of winter, and I was so delighted by the coming of spring and summer that I had forgotten the best was still to come.

On my last visit I had seen not a single dragonfly or butterfly, and assumed that this was it for the year, but I soon find myself being buzzed by a couple of the southern hawker dragonflies that prefer the woods, and there are numerous red admirals, and a solitary late-flying purple hairstreak. This is a lovely little butterfly, and one that I had missed earlier on in the season, for it tends to stay high in the oaks and is difficult to spot. And then I come upon three green woodpeckers; two on the ground and one poised on the trunk of a tree. Having said that I had hardly seen a green woodpecker all year, I'd now been rewarded by seeing three before breakfast.

I walk on through dripping, mushroomy woods, crossing streams in full spate. This is a particularly large expanse of pasture woodland, interspersed with sudden clearings. Some of them are small patches of heathland, some are largely overgrown with bracken, while others are grassy, park-like lawns. I can tell in advance which are grassland from a glance at my map. If the clearing is overgrown then the dotted line marking the footpath continues across it, but if it is grass, then the trail stops at the point where the woods end. You can wander at will, and there becomes no need for a route. The only issue is that, when you reach the far side of the clearing, you may have to hunt about to find the way back into the woods. After a mile or two I come to a huge clearing of many acres, with cattle grazing far off. This is marked on my map as Little Stubby Hat; a name that had already made it into my commonplace book in my list of appealing forest names. These clearings, embedded deep within the woods, and surrounded entirely by trees, are all different from one another; all seem to have their own unique atmosphere, and somehow come as a surprise even when you know you are due to approach one. With their close-cropped grass and the browsing livestock, they look almost like farmer's fields, but for the complete absence of straight edges. They are organic in shape, self-willed, with protruding peninsulas of trees, clumps of woodland islanded across them, and ancient solitaries dotted around seemingly at random.

Setting off across the centre of the clearing, I realise that I am being observed. A roe deer with a fawn just behind her is at the edge of the clearing, and they are keeping pace with me, watchful. As I make my way, they follow me in parallel, but keeping close to the trees at all times. I head to the largest clump for a better look. It is thick with hollies, but with a few ancient oaks at the centre. This is a hat, or a holm, a holly wood; in fact, this is probably the eponymous little stubby hat itself. A growth of hollies establishes itself out on a clearing, no doubt from berries dropped by birds. They have some limited protection against grazers, though ponies will still have a go. After a while, an impenetrable stand of dense holly bushes establishes itself. Into its midst, within shelter, an acorn is dropped, and a sapling gets a chance to thrive within their protection. This is a slow process; the oak trees that have grown here are now hundreds of years old. At the edge of the woods, a tree may fall, opening up the canopy, and the livestock prevent regrowth, so a new area may be absorbed into the clearing. I can imagine what it will look like in years to come; the woods and the clearing pulsing, expanding here, contracting there, reshaping themselves like an amoeba, transforming itself over the time span of centuries.

My map is dotted with the marks of human history dating back thousands of years. A great scattering of tumuli and earthworks and dykes; boiling mounds and marl pits; the sites of former royal hunting lodges; wartime bunkers and airfields and bombing ranges. Even the thousands of marked footpaths may have a history that goes back to unrecorded times. People have always walked, and the routes they have taken have largely been led by the lay of the land. But I have found no map that marks the sites of the forgotten compounds.

Gypsies had lived in the forest for centuries, moving on every day or two though seldom leaving the perimeter of the forest. They were perhaps drawn by their affinity for horses, finding work breaking and trading in ponies, with the skills to make a living from the land, weaving baskets, making pegs and cane chairs and bee skeps, which they could sell to the local cottagers. Indications are that they were fairly well accepted by local residents, whose lives were perhaps, while settled in one place, not all that different; they too were scraping a living from the largesse of the forest. The reformer William Cobbett, when he wrote *Rural Rides* in the 1820s, described the New Forest as the poorest district in the kingdom. Many local people lived in turf huts at the edges of the forest, setting up home by squatting on land that was just outside the forest boundaries, and therefore not subject to forest law. The legacy of this is still visible on today's maps. Where a road marks the forest boundary may be a long, staggered village, such as East Boldre, splayed along one side of the road, while on the other is the open forest. One such village, Nomansland, just over the county border in Wiltshire, was established by Gypsies themselves in around 1740, and survived a legal challenge to prove that it really was no man's land.

This fringe of houses that marks the edge of the common land in so many places, as well as the many towns and cities that seem to circle the forest, growing ever closer, seems to press on the bounds of the forest, ready to burst in, making it feel under constant threat. The forest could never get larger; it has nowhere to go. It could only ever diminish in size. It is extraordinary that it has survived for as long as it has, hemmed in but holding fast.

While Gypsies elsewhere began to adopt the use of vardos – horse-drawn wagons – to enable them to move further and follow patterns of seasonal work, few in the forest did, for they seldom had cause to travel more than a day's walk away, and even the few roads were little more than gravel tracks. Instead they used Gypsy tents of the traditional style, a tarpaulin thrown over a platform of bent wooden rods. If moved on by the keepers, they could simply 'up sticks' in a matter of minutes, and disappear into the trees and on to their next encampment. They knew the forest inside and out; knew every source of fresh spring water. While some families had surnames common to Gypsies nationwide, such as Lee and Smith, there were other family names that were very much of the forest and the neighbouring areas: Stanley and Cooper, Sherrard and Willetts, Eyres and Wells, among others.

If for much of its history the New Forest had been a largely forgotten and self-contained corner of the country, by the Victorian era it was beginning to open up, first with the arrival of the railway, and then, before long, the motor car. W. H. Hudson was already complaining in 1903, when he published *Hampshire Days*, of the swarms of day-trippers arriving in the forest. The live-and-let-live attitude of the locals was not always shared by this influx of incomers, and the long practice of tolerance was soon to come to an abrupt end.

In 1919 the Forestry Commission was established to take charge of the nation's forests, in response to concerns over the level of clearance that had taken place during the Great War, and attitudes towards the Gypsies soon hardened. They were seen as a problem that needed fixing. In 1926, seven compounds were established across the forest, and the Gypsies were effectively rounded up and forced to move into them. They were granted licences that both permitted and compelled them to live in a particular named compound, and this fifty years before any restrictions on camping wild in the forest were applied to anyone other than the Gypsies. Forcing people to live in ghettos solely because of their race is an act that has history, and not an honourable one; it seems incredible that such behaviour continued in the British countryside into my own lifetime.

The residents of the compounds were allowed to expand their tents into makeshift huts, but more established features, such as floors, doors and windows, were prohibited under forest law. The sites were often miles from the nearest water source, and while moving on every couple of days had left little mark on the land, forcing sometimes more than a hundred people to cluster together permanently in a small space often turned the compounds into a quagmire. During the Second World War, some of the sites were moved to make way for airfields and bombing ranges, and after the war, attitudes towards the Gypsies hardened still further; the compounds, into which they had been forced against their will, were seen as a blight on the landscape. Forestry Commission reports of the time actually began to talk of elimination and purges. The residents of the compounds were cajoled, pressurised and finally forced to abandon their way of life, to leave the forest, and to move into the newly built council estates that had mushroomed around the neighbouring cities. In 1963, the final hold-outs, Maurice and Mabel Cooper, were forcibly evicted, and the five-hundred-year history of the Gypsies of the New Forest was brought to a violent end. It is a shameful story that has been largely expunged from the history books.

I have been heading to the site of Shave Green, one of the largest of the former compounds and perhaps the best known, not least because it featured in a couple of Pathé newsreels discussing 'the Gypsy problem'. It would not be possible to find the location unaided – Shave Wood covers a very large area, and it turns out that the site was not actually at Shave Green itself, but a good distance away at Brockis Hill. I am relying on guidance given to me by Gypsy historian Len Smith, who I first met close to two decades ago. He is long gone now, but left behind him a book, *Romany Nevi Wesh: An Informal History of the New Forest Gypsies*.

To get to the site I have to cross the main road that runs north to south between Cadnam and Lyndhurst. There is no evident path into the woods; the verge is overgrown and there is a high fence. It is not that the wood is an enclosure; it is the road that is being fenced here rather than the woodland. Ponies and fast cars do not go well together; there are many casualties every year. I wait for a lull in the traffic to jump the road-side ditch, push my way through the undergrowth, and mount the fence. I find myself on a steep slope thick with hollies. As I climb, I come upon what must once have been a cart track but is impassable nowadays even on foot, criss-crossed as it is by fallen trees. Further uphill, the ground levels, the hollies thin out, and I come upon a wood of ancient beeches. Beeches shade out competitors and little grows underneath them – all that lies beneath is a thick layer of crisp leaf litter. These are some of the finest beeches I have seen in the forest; vast grey columns and a silence that is almost sepulchral. Here was the site of the compound, under these trees but razed clean now to the point of invisibility. There is a certain logic to the site having been placed here; beeches tend to grow where the soil is a little drier. And like most of the compounds, it was tucked away out of view from any roads or houses; out of sight and out of mind.

Brockis Hill certainly lives up to its name; I have never seen so many badger setts, certainly not in the forest, and possibly nowhere else either. But the badgers are sleeping now. Ahead of me beneath the trees stands a tiny spotted fawn. When they are very young, the does will leave them unattended for the day while they go off to graze, relying on them to keep their heads down and make good use of their camouflage. This fawn doesn't seem to have got the memo, though; it totters towards me enthusiastically as if it is expecting me to produce a bottle, only at the last moment thinking better of it and diverting into a nearby stand of dying bracken. There, it instantly becomes almost invisible, even though it is standing right in front of me.

At first it looks like there is absolutely no remaining trace of the generations of people who lived here. But then I sit on the mossy root bole of a splendid beech and soak in the atmosphere, and after a while I get my eye in. A glint among the leaf litter is a half-buried glass bottle, still intact. Then a fragment of earthenware. Then a large crushed can, protruding from the fallen leaves. It is weathered to bare metal now, but when I pull it from the ground and unfold it I can see that it is scarlet. I wipe away the humus and read: *There's nothing like OXO.* It has probably lain here undisturbed for eighty years. It is precious little; it seems as though tremendous effort has been made to erase every last trace of the history of this place. This doesn't feel right to me; there should be some kind of tribute to all those who lived here. A plaque, a memorial, something rather than nothing.

The place feels haunted, missing the voices of

children, the crackle of the yog beneath a bubbling cauldron of joey grey, the whack of firewood being chopped. I know that I bring this haunting with me, and if I walked this fine beech wood with no knowledge of its history, then I would not feel this sense of absence. It feels personal, though I know it isn't, not really. My own antecedents finally left the forest for good over a century ago, before the time of the compounds, and settled in town, explaining away their black hair and dark skin with tales of a Spanish grandmother. The Gypsy Coopers who lived here could likely only have been distant relatives at best. But it feels personal in a different way, like a shutting down of options, a way of life that has been denied to me; to everyone, in fact. It is like following my path through the woods and finding my way barred with fences and shuttered gates and keep-out signs.

Perhaps it should feel personal to all of us. The expulsion of the Gypsies was unfinished business, a tying up of loose ends left over from the Enclosure Acts and the Highland clearances. In a system that celebrates the primacy of the private ownership of land, self-sufficiency is an act of radical non-conformity, a threat to the status quo. We are all brought up to aspire to home ownership. Society expects us to take out a massive loan, and, if we spend our lives working hard enough, we may finally have earned enough to have the rights to our very own tiny plot of land. And this is considered success. Meanwhile the vast landscape around us is all sewn up; a tiny handful of people are born to thousands of acres. This aspiration can be seductive, though, and deeply ingrained; it was certainly my own father's life goal. He was a deeply territorial man by nature, and wherever he lived he seemed to end up sparring with his neighbours. Mostly this would be a cold war of hard stares and silent treatment, but sometimes it would escalate, to lawsuits and even, once, to a street fight.

I, too, have sometimes dreamt of a place all my own, my own little piece of nature where there was no one to tell me what I could or couldn't do. A little cabin would do me just fine; I am not greedy. But then sometimes I think, no, that is just a pipe dream, I am too much of a wanderer to ever really feel settled in one place. And the reality for most of us is that we live where we have to, not where we want to, or at most settle for the best compromise we can afford. We are taught to feel that private ownership is the natural order of things, but really it is just one among many ways of sharing our resources, has been largely imposed on us, and is a fairly recent development. It is only in the last century or so that mass home-ownership has been regarded as the norm to which we should all aspire – and though it is easy to assume that the way things are is the way things have to be, it is not necessarily so. In fact, private property is a relatively new paradigm when you take a longer view of humanity, one that ultimately serves the purposes of those very few people who hold all the cards, who have the most to gain and the most to lose. In the meantime, we are bought off with the promise that maybe, one day, we too could have the merest sliver of the pie.

FIFTEEN

Bullet Fee

October 2019

Not all of the Coopers were poor. So says my mother, almost the moment we start our phone conversation. I don't normally like sharing my work in progress, or even talking about it, but my mother has always been the one person who encouraged me in my ambitions to write, and as I am talking a little about my early life you could say she has a vested interest in this particular piece of writing. Family history is not just one person's alone to tell; it is shared history, and often enough it is contested history. People's memories differ, and their perspectives, and their priorities. So, every time I have a few more chapters drafted I send them off to her in a batch, and she will often open our next conversation with her comments, as often as not her thoughts on something

I could have included, but haven't. I am sure it is true, I say, that we had relatives who did well for themselves and who were well off, as I am sure is true of any family, but these supposedly rich Coopers do not include any of my antecedents, nor anyone close enough for me to ever have met them, nor even be able to put a name to them.

Writing a memoir can be a minefield. Do you leave someone out of the story, out of discretion, or do you include them, and perhaps anonymise them, or do you go all out and name them? People may variously be offended that they have been left out, that they have been included, that they have been named, that they have not been named. I have circumvented a lot of problems in the past by the very fact that my memoirs have largely focused on me, alone, among the birds – and birds make no complaints. But life is not lived entirely in isolation. Sometimes you cannot help but find yourself trampling on someone else's lawn.

I talk to my mother about the difference between memoir and autobiography. In autobiography, the author is the subject of the story, but not so in a memoir; a memoir is outward-looking, the point is to harness your experience of things outside yourself. The fact that you remember something does not mean it automatically should be included; it is not a grab-bag of everything you happen to recall. Memoir is targeted recollection, memory curated, used in service of a broader goal.

The next time I talk to my mother, she says to me, apropos of nothing: You should tell them I was a dancer. It is true, my mother, who now has severe difficulty getting about at all, was a dancer when she was young. She had some success at it too; I can just remember a glass-fronted cabinet filled with trophies. And then, of course, she got married, and never danced again. On another call some time ago she said: I hope you're going to tell them about Fred. I told her Fred wasn't really relevant to what I'm trying to write a book about, and she accepted this reluctantly. But what the hell. Fred was my pet chicken. She was the sole hatchling in an incubator in the biology lab at school, and was named Fred before we knew she was a hen rather than a cockerel. She never met another chicken in her life, and no doubt thought she was human. She spent most of her days on the doorstep pecking at the letterbox, and defending the house against intruders, such as postmen and milkmen. She was a guard chicken. If you were not careful when you opened the door, she would dive in, race around the house, and jump into a bed. She enjoyed climbing trees, but only upwards. A ladder was frequently required. Eventually a fox got her.

I am sending my mother instalments of a book that includes some small elements of shared history, so it is bound to trigger her own recollections, elements of what she might have chosen to include in her own memoir, were she ever to have written one. I was surprised, though, that when it came to the one tranche of memories that I had thought might be particularly subjective and in need of revision, she had nothing to add. When it came to the time of the fire, she said only that she was amazed that I could remember it in such detail and so accurately, considering that I was so young at the time. She found for me a clip from the local paper from back in the sixties, a report on our fire. One column inch.

Yesterday it rained all day. Tomorrow, it will rain all day too, if the weather forecast is to be believed. And the rest of the week too. But today the sun is shining, between great pillows of cloud. It is one of those crisp, clear autumn days where the chill of the night lingers on into morning. I am on Setley Plain, not far from Brockenhurst, searching for traces of the wartime prisoner-of-war camp. It is much easier to find than the Shave Green Gypsy compound. The area where the camp had been is overgrown now, with furze, with bracken, but mostly with brambles. I presume the site must have been fenced off from livestock for long enough for the scrub to take hold. The rabbits must like the cover of the brambles, for there are pellets everywhere, far more than I have seen elsewhere in the forest. I spot fox scats too, and then, beneath a solitary pine, a dozen little pits: badger latrines. There has been a lot of digesting going on around here. First come the rabbits, and then the predators are not far behind.

There are chunks of crumbling concrete debris, sometimes with blocks of bricks still attached. Also, sections of earthenware drainage pipes embedded in the earth. I feel like an archaeologist as I scour the site, though if it is this hard to make sense of the leftover traces from seventy years ago, I cannot help but feel a great deal of admiration for those having to interpret remains that date back millennia. Then I find a square of concrete flush with the surface of the earth, and in its

centre a round hole. A flagpole once stood here, I deter-
mine, and I feel slightly impressed with myself. There is
no trace of the buildings themselves, for the prisoners
were housed in long-ago dismantled Nissen huts that
looked like corrugated-steel polytunnels. During the
early part of the war, the camp housed Italian prisoners
deemed low risk, who were sent out to work each day as
foresters or farm labourers. After the Italian armistice in
1943, they were replaced by German prisoners of war
in their stead. And then, after the war was over, and a
prison camp was surplus to requirements, they used
the place for Gypsies. Of course they did.

I follow animal trails that wind through the scrub. A
Dartford warbler – a fuzzacker – darts from gorse bush
to gorse bush. A woodlark flushes from the heather at
my feet and soars above me briefly before dropping back
down into cover. I've only just arrived in the forest
and have already seen two birds that would have been
notable sightings for me had I not been coming here
all year. I head across the more open expanses of the
heath towards the woods. At the edge of the heath is a
profusion of parasol mushrooms, the smaller ones
like bulbs, and the fully grown ones like mottled, scaly

dish-plates. The woods are filled with great glowing masses of sulphur tuft toadstools, and I spot a cep or penny-bun, my first this year, possibly the best of all eating mushrooms and one that I used to hunt for in the forests of Sweden.

Travelling on, I come to Hincheslea Bog, a long valley surrounded by woodland and a seemingly textbook example of a New Forest valley mire. The middle of the valley is thick with reed beds, fringed with alder carr and great swathes of bog myrtle. There is a trail that leads right across the centre of the bog. In the middle are broad patches of open water, slow moving. The sunshine glints off the barest trickle of the waters, and the pools reflect the roiling clouds above. I pause and look down at the image of the sky above reflected in the clear waters. Is there anything more beautiful? I find a leaning willow that makes a perfect bench for me to sit on and take it all in. Willows are generous like that; they are among the most horizontal of trees. There are reed buntings flittering through the reeds, and a grey wagtail bobbing at the water's edge. The name grey wagtail hardly does it justice; its breast and rump are a glorious lemon yellow. But the name yellow wagtail was already taken. Today, on this fine autumn morning, it feels like a place of ineffable peace and beauty. Such impressions are of the moment, I suppose; on a bleak, grey day the effect would be very different, and I might have passed by without giving it its due. Darters are swarming all around. It seems late in the year for dragonflies, but these have a trick that carries them into the autumn; they pause regularly and sun themselves, to give themselves that little bit more energy, which enables them to outlast most of their relatives when the temperatures begin to fall. One stops to soak up the sunshine on the willow trunk right beside me, just inches away, and gives me the opportunity to examine it in detail. A common darter, nothing special perhaps, but it bears close scrutiny nevertheless. Dragonflies are usually off in a moment. Its long body is a glorious orange-red, with a few black dots and stripes, its eyes are a deep reddish brown, and the dark red legs have a pale, lemony line right along their length. It is perfectly symmetrical, with each segment of its body marked by two matching black dots. Metallic-looking, it appears armoured, as if it has been assembled by a crew of tiny sheet-metal workers and pop-riveted together. Its four wings are glassy and transparent, like a chequerboard of black-framed panes. Each wing has a single rectangular pane, which is a brilliant red too, each at the leading edge. Most things I see for just a fleeting moment; this is a useful reminder that even a seemingly humble creature can have hidden depths that could so easily elude me. Everything benefits from a closer look.

I walk back towards Brockenhurst. The villages of the New Forest lie outside the perambulation of the national park, and are mostly surrounded by a buffer zone of farmers' fields, of hedges and fences. It stands to reason, as the commoners need to hold on to a bit of pastureland for when they move their animals off the open forest. It does create a curious effect, however. It means that in a single step you can be transported from a landscape characteristic of the common lands of the New Forest to one that could be anywhere in England. It is like being suddenly transported into the English countryside, having been somewhere quite distinctively other. Grassy fields, fences, gates, a perfectly delineated copse of trees, a footpath – if you are lucky enough that people in past times have fought for it. Markers of ownership every-where: mine, mine, mine. This is not to say that England does not contain pockets of great beauty, but for the most part we live in a constructed landscape, in the country as much as in the city. Almost the only places where there is more of a self-willed landscape are where things have been abandoned and left to their own devices, and they have returned to nature without human intervention, those neglected spaces that are neither town nor country. The edgelands, as they were first called by Marion Shoard, author in the eighties of the books *This Land is our Land* and *The Theft of the Countryside*. I think her book titles make it fairly clear where she was coming from. A woman after my own heart, or perhaps I should say that I am a man after her own heart, as she came first.

It is always a comfort to hear of conservation successes. People can be hugely dedicated and passionate when it comes to saving something they care about – a particular threatened species or a specific small habitat at risk. There are clear goals and limits, and success or failure can be measured. It is always a relief when something is brought back from the brink of disappearing altogether. And yet the bigger picture remains inescapable; we are living in a country that has only half the number of birds and perhaps a quarter the number of flying insects that it did when I was a child, just a generation ago. What are we leaving the next generation, or the one after that? Everything is connected to everything else. We are all living in one giant nature reserve; it is big and it is round, and it is all that we have.

The vast majority of our countryside is homogenised, stripped of diversity, poisoned with pesticides and fertilisers. Productivity is measured only in money. We need to rewild at least a significant portion of that land. But how can this be done when practically all of the land is owned by just a handful of people, whose land is their wealth? And it is not enough just to leave it fallow and untouched. You could abandon the Highlands of Scotland to their own devices, and yet the forests would never grow back when there are no predators left to control the numbers of deer. An ecosystem only functions naturally if you restore entire food chains, and yet an awful lot of people seem to go into conniptions at the slightest suggestion of the return of predators. Rewilding requires human intervention, and intervention requires hard choices. If we are to attempt to restore the land to a state before the current levels of human interference, just what period are we looking at? Five hundred years ago? A thousand years ago? Ten thousand years ago? This country was swept almost clean of life by the last era of glaciation, and what remained after the retreat of the ice was little more than a blank slate – in some places literally blank slate. People returned to these shores pretty much at the same time as the rest of life. There was no prelapsarian Eden here. Do we return predators that became extinct only in the last millennium, or predators that became extinct when people here were still largely hunter-gatherers? Do we eliminate all non-native species? What even is a non-native species? The fallow deer was introduced by the Normans, and probably before that in smaller numbers by the Romans. But apparently the fossil record shows that it was in fact once native here; before the ice came. Does that even count?

We need to reintroduce lost species, because we are an island, and they cannot just drift back in of their own accord when conditions improve, as they have begun to do in some other European countries. But beyond that, the idea of restoring the land to an imagined golden age is an unrealistic one, as it would require constant human intervention. Perhaps, as George Monbiot points out in his book *Feral*, rewilding needs to be more about surrendering control of the land than a form of conservation, and driven by natural processes rather than human management, without a fixed goal in mind.

Fundamentally, we are in a position where we can no longer do nothing, if we don't want the natural world around us to degrade still further. Many of the major rewilding projects that currently exist depend substantially on the goodwill of a few major landowners. They may have the best of intentions, but they are a small minority, and relying on them cannot be an effective long-term strategy. We have essentially been paying landowners to ruin the land, through agricultural subsidies. Most of these subsidies don't go to small farmers, who may need them to survive. Rather, they are hoovered up by industrial-scale farming and major landowners. Many of the really large estates that take agricultural subsidies are barely what you or I would consider a farm at all – moors for driven grouse-shooting, or deer forests for stalking, that somehow contrive to be eligible for agricultural subsidies, but not eligible for business taxes. The fact is that we are still living in what is largely a feudal system, thinly disguised under a wisp of democracy, but designed to work primarily in the interests of a handful of the privileged, entitled by birth and history. We would be better off paying these land-owners to improve the environment rather than destroy it, on a scale vastly larger than those presently being tried. Subsidising the protection and hopefully the improvement of our environment rather than simply production may ultimately be the most realistic way forward, and seems to be the way the world is headed. It does tend to stick in the craw, though. First they steal the land, then they drive us off the land, then they make us pay them to fuck it up, and now it seems that the only way we can get them to stop is to pay them again. It puts one in mind of the bullet fee, by which certain govern-ments have supposedly been known to send people a bill, to cover the cost of the bullets used to execute their family members.

It seems to me that one thing we need alongside rewilding is a measure of re-commoning, to restore greater land rights to everyone, so that people feel more invested in the land, more connected. An experiment akin to re-commoning is being undertaken in the Highlands and Islands of Scotland, where land ownership is even more concentrated in the hands of a tiny minority than it is in England. There, when tracts of land do occasionally come to market, the policy in the first instance is that it should be offered for a community buyout before it goes to another private landowner. More like this, please, on a much bigger scale. And Scotland, too, has a right to roam. We have a long way to go to catch up with them, here in England. Reading Marion Shoard, it seems to me there has been a millennium-long struggle between the landed and the landless, a battle that never ends. We may occasionally extract a small concession, and feel that we have won a skirmish, for example, rescuing the right of way along a threatened footpath. But the more you think about land ownership, the more unjust it begins to seem. You can inherit a large plot of land, and make a good living entirely by charging rents for people to make use of that land. You do not need to put an ounce of effort into it – you could do this without even once visiting 'your' plot. You contribute absolutely nothing beyond a title deed. As the early environmentalist Aldo Leopold explained it in his book *A Sand County Almanac*, conservation will get nowhere for as long as we continue to treat the land as a commodity, rather than a community.

Over the past hundred years much of our rural landscape has changed from one of small family farms, of small fields interspersed with hedges and copses, to what looks more like a prairie. Long ago, before the time of the enclosures, landowners at least accepted that with their rights came a certain amount of responsibility towards the landless. But the assumption has increasingly become that ownership is absolute, that nothing should stand in the way of an entitlement to extract every last penny from the land, come what may. Grubbing out hedgerows? Fine. Ploughing up a wild-flower meadow? Fine. Draining a wetland? Fine. Showering your land with toxic chemicals? Every little helps. Planting a block of Christmas trees on unproductive heathland? Also fine. And if clearing woodland and straightening streams results in flooding downstream, then that's some-body else's problem. Similarly, if birds and animals are spiralling into decline as a result of such practices, then so be it; they have no monetary value and just get in the way of business. There are a tiny proportion of land-owners who have thought carefully about environmental stewardship; a fine example would be the owners of the

Knepp Estate in Sussex, as described in Isabella Tree's book *Wilding*. But these remain very much the exception. And yet the attitude that what's mine is mine, and nobody else has any business in having an opinion in what I do, is hardly supportable, especially when landowners are entirely reliant on subsidies paid for by us and our tax contributions. It is not an assumption that is made in other areas. If we buy a house and garden, we accept that, if we want to build an extension, we will have to make a planning application, and it will have to be in keeping with the local plans. We understand that, if we make so much noise that it bothers the neighbours, then we may end up with a noise abatement notice. We have a duty to each other, and to the interests of the world in which we live. One of Marion Shoard's principal recommendations was that planning permission should be extended from changes to buildings to changes in agricultural use. At the moment the Town and Country Planning Act involves an awful lot of town planning, and precious little country planning.

We have perhaps too much of a binary outlook on the world. We either exploit it to extract the maximum profit out of it or we think that it should be left entirely alone in the hands of nature, an untouched wilderness. A place like the New Forest demonstrates that it is perhaps possible to engage with the earth in a way that benefits us yet doesn't turn it into a wasteland. We have our place in the world, but we need to recognise that we live in a shared space. If someone has control of a tract of land, they need to be asking how they can occupy it and, if necessary, live off it, while causing the least possible harm. And this is much more likely to happen when we are occupying a shared space, and are answerable to one another, and thus can create checks on individual greed.

We live in temperate climes; not too hot and dry, yet less cold than they might be at this latitude, warmed by the wet winds driven by the Gulf Stream. Although recent years may have pushed at the limits of this moderation, we are still likely to be hit slightly less hard by climate change than more extreme environments. We live in a region that should be eminently suitable for a vast array of living creatures to inhabit, but the land has been ravaged in a race to the bottom. There has been a great thinning, a great devouring, and it has largely been for the benefit of a very small minority. When I walk in this forest, I don't just see a fragmentary relic of a past way of life, a road that was abandoned long ago. I see a landscape rich in life that looks a lot like what much of our countryside should by rights resemble. Not just a possible past, but a possible future too, if only we were able to envisage a better way of being.

SIXTEEN

The Stormcock Sings

November–December 2019

By the beginning of November, the call of autumn is in full throat. The oaks have now joined the beeches and the birches, and everything is on the turn. Yet the mass of leaves has yet to fall, so the woods are a patchwork quilt of green and gold, of copper and red and orange and brown and lemon. In today's sunshine they are radiant, glowing with reflected light. As I crunch through them they are silent, though, compared to the bustle of summer. The bird life of the woods has thinned right out, and almost all that is left are the stalwarts; the blackbird kicking through the fallen leaves and the robin hopping from shrub to shrub. There is the sudden cronk of a raven; I look up and see it right above me, passing just above the canopy. It has clearly spotted me.

I am wandering off trail, following the colours. Dotted through these woods, amongst the plentiful staples of oak and beech and birch, are a handful of field maples. For most of the year this tree passes almost unnoticed; I am much more likely to notice the occasional crab apple or rowan. It is infrequent and not a particularly large or otherwise remarkable tree. Even though it may live for as long as the forest giants it will never reach a fraction of their size. Then autumn comes, and it finally has its moment, and the little fleur-de-lis leaves turn at once to the most glorious buttercup yellow. Later in the season its leaves may turn again, to red or purple. It glows golden in the distance, and each time I reach one it seems that I can just make out the next one far away through the woods, like a beacon leading me on.

While so many birds have flown, the fungi at least are revealing themselves to full effect. The first crop that I had seen on recent visits has now swollen to full fruition. There has been no shortage of rain this season, and I don't think I have ever seen such a profusion of mushrooms and toadstools. A whole hidden world of life that is briefly revealed to us. Everywhere are *Lactarius* species – the milkcaps – and *Russula* species – the brittlegills –

in an array of colours: red and yellow, mauve and purple, green and brown. There are the inevitable fly agarics, the archetypal woodland toadstool, but other *Amanitas* too, such as the lovely-looking panther cap, in a rich caramel brown. There are long trails of wood hedgehog mushrooms, with soft spines instead of gills, and among them the wonderfully named terracotta hedgehog. And encircling the moss at the foot of a beech, I come upon a great swarm of the winter chanterelle – the yellowfoot. You don't come across them often, but when you do they come in the hundreds, or even the thousands. So if I am not following the glow of the distant maples, I am tracking the glint of another exotic-looking mushroom amongst the leaf litter. Most of them I am completely unable to identify. I am probably walking in circles, having totally lost any sense of a route.

I come to the edge of the woods, to a large grassy clearing. The raven calls again right above me, to its mate away across the clearing; a charm of goldfinches blows over, and a pied wagtail – a polly dishwasher – is bobbing on the grass. Standing proud of the woods is a giant of an oak. It is out on a limb, you might say; it looks like it is on the move, breaking free of the woods and making its way out into the clearing. There is a sudden gust of wind, and a shower of leaves cascades all around me, twirling in the breeze. I drop everything and dance around like an idiot, trying to catch one single leaf before it reaches the ground. Everybody does this, don't they? It's a tradition, surely, though not perhaps among sensible grown-ups. It is not as easy as you might think. Catching falling leaves is like catching butterflies. Each time I try to snatch one from the air, it seems to change direction at the very last moment, as if it has a will of its own. With a final lunge, I manage to get one in my grasp. It is crisp and brittle and copper-brown, and now I have it in my hand I don't quite know what to do with it. I slip it into my jeans pocket, where it will crumble into dust.

I had hoped to take full advantage of the beauty of the season, and planned to return almost immediately for an epic woodland walk. But it was not to be; my mother was taken ill, and my train journeys became hospital visits. Just recently, I had sent her another batch of chapters for her perusal. I had forwarded them to her with a degree of reticence, wondering if incorporating our ongoing telephone conversations into my writing would be a step too far, something too close to an invasion of privacy. I assumed that, being seriously unwell, she would have other things on her mind, but not at all; not only had she read them but they were one of the first things she wanted to talk about. It is very accurate, she says, and the book is getting better and better as it goes on. As, I suppose, I tunnel deeper into my thoughts, and share a little more of our shared history. I can see she is becoming more and more committed to this book, and wants to see it through to the end as much as I do. And she is not offended at all by my publicising our private phone calls. It is as if a book that began as a conversation with myself is starting to become a conversation with my mother.

I have worked in the past as a news journalist, and one of the first rules of journalism is that you never surrender editorial control. If you interview a politician, and then allow them to take a look at and pass comment on what you are going to say before you have said it, you are no longer a journalist; you have become a publicist. Sharing my work in progress is therefore not something that comes naturally. But, inspired by how well my mother has responded to what, to me as a memoirist, feels like a fairly radical exercise in shared participation,

I decide it is time I showed my children the chapter in which they appear. My daughter Kaya quickly emails me my very first review, even though she is in the next room. And here it is, minus the emojis:

> I loved the chapter! Was really nice to see your thoughts and to remember a lovely day. It's personal yet informative, and nostalgic and humorous, but most of all I would say heart-warming. I like how you talk about us and then your own childhood with your dad and then about the bird being a dutiful parent to its young. The bit about us running away from the snake sound made me laugh loads. I do not appreciate your groan at the end of our wonderful joke!

My mother seems to be spending a lot of her time these days looking through old photographs. I suppose she has reached a point in her life when the past means more than the present; the age of summing up, of trying to take the measure of everything. She shows a little snap of me taken in the sixties that I don't recall having seen before. I am, I suppose, about six or seven years old. Grey shorts above spindly legs, socks and sandals, bowl-cut hair. This photo was unquestionably taken in the New Forest, from a visit I can no longer remember. There is a herd of New Forest ponies grazing a close-cropped lawn, and behind them a gorse brake and then, further away, a bank of trees on the horizon. I rather like the picture; I like that my back is to the camera. It is not really a picture of me, it is a picture of the ponies, and I just happen to have got in the way, looking at the world around me rather than looking to the camera.

I was always closer to my mother than my father. My father was never an easy man, and it was only really in his later years that he began to mellow a little, and we were able to rebuild bridges. My parents were very much a product of their times. Theirs was a fifties marriage; the husband would come home from work and expect to find his dinner on the table. Childcare was entirely and absolutely women's work. As the times moved on, he resisted change because, well, why wouldn't he? When I was very young, he went through a long spell of unemployment, and when the days were at their bleak-est – no money in the bank, no food in the cupboard – he would go out on suburban hunting expeditions, taking an air rifle and shooting the wood pigeons out of the trees in the garden. I don't remember this, but he would cite it sometimes as evidence that he would do whatever it took to support his family. I think, because he grew up in poverty, and had known hard times and felt their sting, he was always aware of the wolf at the door, or at least nearby, hiding in the woods and biding its time.

As a child, I had always been perplexed by my father's reaction to the fire. He seemed excited by it, almost as though it was a game. And then, after that grim nine or ten months of homelessness, our family fortunes seemed to take a marked turn for the better, as though we had taken a step up in the world. I found it difficult to trust my father – his unpredictable moods made me wary of him, and I harboured suspicions that the fire had not been an accident, but rather had been part of a master-plan; that this was my father doing whatever it took to support his family, as he put it. As I grew up to become a rebellious teenager, my suspicions that the fire had in reality been arson in pursuit of an insurance settlement hardened into a conviction, a conviction that did nothing for the atmosphere at home, and was no doubt part of the reason why I determined to leave home for good as soon as was feasibly possible, and get as far away as I was able. Now, I no longer know quite what to think. Perhaps my father's uncharacteristic cheerfulness over the fate that had befallen us was simply his way of trying to keep our spirits up. And perhaps all the financial benefits that seemed to flow our way as a result of the fire were merely my father making the best of a bad situation. Whatever the truth of the matter, there is no doubt that it shaped my childhood, and perhaps the person I have become; the feeling that home is not a place that you turn to for safety and comfort, but rather true comfort is to be found out there, in the woods and fields. Nature felt more reliable than people.

By the time I finally make it back to the forest more than three weeks have passed; the longest absence I have had from it all year. I am beginning to feel almost a sense of withdrawal. It is as if these regular visits are what give my life meaning. Whenever I go for long without getting out in nature I start to feel an ache, a void in my life. It has always been thus, and this year at least, nature means the forest. December has come, and the cold with it. It is no longer autumn, it is very decidedly winter. The change since last month is immense. Almost all the leaves have fallen from the trees, and that great harvest of fungi is almost over. The few toadstools left standing are mostly crumbling from the frost.

For all the recent storms, it is one of those wonderfully clear, crisp winter days, rather like my first visit of the year way back in January. That seems an awfully long time ago now. A lot of miles have been walked since then, a lot of birds have been watched, trees sheltered under, bridges paused on, and thoughts thought. The sky is an unbroken blue. Out on the heath the pools are covered with a crazy-paving of ice. The sun feels warm against my face, but in the shade the chill of the night remains, and the fallen leaves are all limned with a tracery of sparkling hoar frost that seems to give them a second life. There is a satisfying crunch as I walk under the trees where the sunshine has not touched the ground. Already, by early afternoon, the sun has fallen below the treetops. It glints through the branches and sends the shadows of the trees stretching far out across the heath. Above the dead and fallen bracken at the woodland edge is a vast swarm of tiny flies. They would undoubtedly have escaped my notice were they not lit up by the horizontal light. I am not the only one to have seen them. A flock of little green-and-yellow goldcrests has come to feast on them. With them are a couple of camp-followers – wrens. Tiny prey for tiny predators.

In the branches of a dying tree I spot a pair of small black-and-white birds scuttling along the branches. They are barely bigger than sparrows. Lesser spotted woodpeckers, by far the scarcest of our woodpecker species, a hundred times less numerous than their bigger cousins, as well as far more inconspicuous. They have eluded me all year, even though I knew they were resident here in the forest, even though I knew they were reputedly present in this very wood, which I have visited repeatedly. I am delighted to have found them at last, for their population has suffered a rapid decline, and it is a relief to know that they are still holding on here. A moment later, I see a great spotted woodpecker in a neighbouring tree, and it looks massive in comparison. And then, soon after, there is a sudden chuckle, and a yaffle, a green woodpecker, flies up from the ground. All of our three woodpeckers in as many minutes. This is the nature of the winter woods; for a long time you see nothing, and then you are suddenly surrounded by life.

I notice a couple of small thrushes flying from the

ground up into the trees, and then they are followed by more, rising up in twos and threes. As I look closer I see that the trees are actually filled with thrushes. They pick through one tree and the ground beneath it, then all pass on to the next. Working the wood. My first flock this year of redwings, winter visitors from Scandinavia. There must be well over a hundred of them, in constant motion. I leave them to it, and set off, away from the woods and across the heath.

The last time I walked this way was in late summer, similarly in the last hours of daylight, and I found myself surrounded by a great assembly of swallows, gathered in readiness for their imminent departure. They circled around me, skimming the ground so close by that they almost touched me as they passed. They dropped, twittering, into a lone hawthorn bush ahead of me, and then as I approached, all lit up together, and began their restless circuit again. It was as if they were leading me on, my retinue. I wondered then if they might draw in a hobby, but it was not to be. Those swallows, and the hobbies too, will be far away now, beyond the Sahara.

As I head my way up a gentle slope towards an isolated copse of oaks far out on the heath, I catch sight of something from the corner of my eye. A falcon flying low and slow alongside me. It is incredibly close, not twenty feet away, and barely above shoulder height. To an observer I would look like a falconer. I can stare right into its eye, see every detail of its black, helmeted head. This is not a hobby, of course, but its bigger cousin the peregrine. It is a male, a tiercel, I can tell from its size; as with most birds of prey, the female is significantly larger than the male. He is clearly not hunting; his flight is slow and leisurely, with a few faint flickers of his wings followed by a slow glide. He has probably just fed. Having come from the same direction as me, he may have encountered the same flock of redwings that I did, and fed among them. Just like the swallows of summer, he apparently has such confidence in his powers of flight that he does not see me as a threat of any kind.

He locks eyes with me, then gradually begins to pull ahead. He is clearly aiming for the same stand of oaks that I am. Just before he reaches the trees, he drops, banks, and describes a perfect anticlockwise circle right at ground level; so tight to the ground that the pointed tip of his right wing brushes the tips of the heather. It is like watching a figure skater; a perfect ten. Then he swoops almost vertically upwards and settles in one of the oaks and begins to preen.

As I close the gap between him and me, a pair of carrion crows fly in. I assume that they have spotted the falcon and have come to mob him, but I am mistaken. They settle in the tree next to his, apparently oblivious. As I reach the edge of the copse, the falcon lifts off, and the crows visibly flinch; it is as if their heads suddenly drop into their shoulders. They look at one another, as if to say: Wait a minute, did you see that? As I pass beneath their tree, they do not take flight, but rather let me come right by them, clearly more bothered by the risk they had just missed with their inattentiveness than by my presence down on the ground beneath them.

Though it feels very much like winter is here, the solstice marking the official start of the season has not yet passed. Even so, I have had my first intimation of spring, like a glimpse into the future. Last night I heard the stormcock sing. I was alone in my flat, late in the evening, hours after nightfall, when I thought I could hear the sound of a bird singing. In all the years I have been here, I don't think I have ever heard a bird singing from inside my flat, save for the cries of the gulls, which don't count. I went out onto the public balcony that runs along the front of the block. The rain was sheeting down, the wind was gusting furiously, and I could hear the hiss of traffic on the wet roads. The rain blew hard into my face, but, overwhelming all this, a bird was singing with immense power and beauty. A short phrase, repeated over and over in great bursts of energy, but each time a little different from the last. Variations on a theme. I looked to the tops of the very few nearby trees to try to spot the singer, but could not make it out in the darkness. It was unmistakably a mistle thrush, known as a storm-cock for its habit of singing through the wildest of storms. This bird is an early singer – it usually begins in February or even the end of January – but to hear one now, the first I have ever heard here in town, before even the solstice, seems improbable and extraordinary. I stand long in the rain, soaking it in, a solitary stormcock singing its heart out through the darkness, by lamplight. It sounds like defiance.

SEVENTEEN

The Torrent

December 2019

It is one of those grey winter days, dark and overcast and still, when you almost need to keep your lights on the whole time. On days like this the countryside can seem almost empty of life. No birds sing, and the migrants have all flown. When we think of migrants, we tend to think of our summer arrivals, the swallows and swifts and cuckoos and warblers, but in fact it is probably true that there are more migrant birds in Britain in the winter than there are in the summer. It is just that the vast majority of them are on the coast. Every autumn, ducks and geese and winter waders arrive in their millions, from Iceland and Greenland, from Lapland and Siberia.

As a child, while I spent my summers wandering the

downs and the woods, in the winter I would head for the marshes, close enough that I could see them from my window. For years I held to the habit of getting up early on New Year's Day, and walking down to Farlington Marshes before anybody else arrived, the dog-walkers and birders, so that I could have the place to myself, and perhaps see things before they had a chance to be disturbed: the hares playing in the fields, or the short-eared owls quartering the saltmarsh. And so, today, I am heading to the coast in the New Forest. The forest has about twenty-five miles of coastline, and I am coming to a part of it that I can remember from when I was young. But my journey has been a disaster; cancelled trains, delayed trains, missed connections. By the time I reach the shore, there is only half an hour left before sunset. I have come to the Keyhaven and Pennington Marshes, a nature reserve near Lymington that is part of the national park. The coastal walk follows the sea wall: mudflats to one side, and on the other saltmarsh, with a series of large shallow lagoons. These are salterns, seawater pools of varying levels of salinity, that were created to evaporate away, leaving the salt exposed. They were salt farms, in effect, but now form a perfect environment for all the waterbirds to retreat to when the tide is high.

The tide is out when I arrive, and though the pools are surrounded by large numbers of winter ducks, of wigeon and teal, and many hundreds of lapwings, whose strange oar-shaped wings flash black and white as groups of them fly from one spot to another, most of the waders are dotted about out on the exposed mudflats. Curlews call continually, that most evocative of all bird calls, and redshanks are skittering about, in perpetual motion. Curlews, redshanks and lapwings; all three of these birds still nest in small numbers in the New Forest, but here, in a single sweep of the eye, I can see more than the entire nesting population of the forest.

Considering that it is so late in the day, and such a dull day at that, the sea wall is still busy with people, mainly dog-walkers, though most are leaving rather than arriving, as I am. As the sun sets invisibly behind thick grey clouds, I stop and sit. Where the sea wall turns at a right angle is a bench; just a single backless construction made from a railway sleeper, but embedded in it are a series of small oval plaques embossed with people's names. Close in on the mudflats beyond are a group of about thirty little black brent geese, proceeding in stately fashion. These are birds that were constant companions on my childhood visits to the marshes in Langstone Harbour along the coast, and being here makes me feel an instant connection to my twelve-year-old self. A flight of oystercatchers passes, piping noisily, and a solitary grey plover stands patiently in the mud. Out with the geese is another solitary wader, paddling through the shallows of a winding rivulet and probing furiously. It is an elegant little bird. Winter waders are not always easy to identify. This bird is bigger than a redshank, pale and slender. It is a greenshank, a pleasure to see as only a few hundred overwinter in Britain, so it is not something I was expecting. Usually they are lost in the throngs of other, commoner birds that look not dissimilar at a distance, but here, although the mudflats stretch out for hundreds of yards into the distance, this one is so close in to shore that I don't even need binoculars to get a perfect view, let alone the telescope that a proper birdwatcher would have brought. I think that I will always be able to pick them out in future; they seem to have a character all their own. Truth be told, I am really not all that skilled in bird identification, when it comes to more challenging groups, such as winter waders or juvenile gulls – at least not compared to many more dedicated birders. It is a question of intent, I think. I watch birds because I like them, not because I am in pursuit of rarity. Some birders will only consider it a good day if they spot a species they have never seen before, and will dedicate themselves to studying the minor differences in plumage that might mark out a rare vagrant. I just want to see something beautiful or fascinating.

On the horizon, beyond the vast expanse of mud and across the Solent, I can see the chalk hills of the Isle of Wight, ending in the white cliffs and stacks of the Needles, and finally their lighthouse. I am content, even though my day's walking has been drastically curtailed. A group of five people approach along the sea wall, and a woman steps forward, apologises for disturbing me, and asks if I can budge along a little. She wants to show her companions the name-plates for her parents. She used to sit here with them, she tells me. She looks out to sea and remarks on how peaceful it is here.

I walk on until it is too dark to see the birds any more, and then make my way back along a country lane in the general direction of Lymington and the railway station.

The lane is completely flooded; in places there is only a narrow strip of tarmac a few inches wide on which I can walk. Fortunately, the still water reflects the last remaining light in the sky, so I can find my way without having to wade in the water at all. As I walk, I am skimmed by a bat, flying back and forth, back and forth above the lane, just at head height. It should be hibernating, and I wonder if it is late to bed or early to rise. Stormcocks singing, and bats on the wing; it seems as though the seasons are out of kilter, as though all the signs that we use to mark the turning of the earth can no longer be relied on.

In the four years from the seventies for which I have written records, I can see that I came here to the New Forest coastline five times in all. Apart from one single winter visit, this was always in high summer, though, when the coast is more of a draw for people, but for birds, not so much. My diaries do tell me, however, that it was here that I came across my first ever Mediterranean gull, and my first ever little ringed plover. I can't recall these two sightings now. Some experiences lodge in the mind and stay there, while others fade away with time.

I guess that the quality of the experience beats novelty, for me at least.

I did come here once this summer, for old times' sake. It was during the dog days of August, and what turned out to be perhaps the hottest day of the year, so that the pools shimmered beneath the heat. The day being long, I could walk further along the sea wall than I would ever have time for in winter. There were inevitably far fewer birds about. A little egret was stalking in the shallows, its head stretched out just above the surface of the water. It moved with infinite patience, raising one leg slowly, ever so slowly, so that there were no drips to disturb its prey. Then it would slowly, ever so slowly, lower that leg a little further forward before raising the other. It was a picture of intense concentration. And then, suddenly, it lost its cool; racing forward, flapping its wings crazily, and jabbing wildly with its bill. All to no avail. It straightened up, shook its feathers back into shape, spotted me watching it from close by, and froze. We locked eyes. It had no expression whatsoever, of course, but I couldn't help but think it looked embarrassed. It was comical.

Little flocks of turnstones poked about among the

rocks at the foot of the sea wall. Compared to other wading birds, they always seem to be remarkably confiding, allowing you to come within just a few feet before scurrying on a little further. And out on the lagoons were hundreds of godwits, all seemingly motionless. Early migrants, I supposed, from Iceland and the Arctic, or perhaps just passing through, stopping over for a break before heading across the Channel. There were few other waders about, and few ducks either. The most visible were the resident shelducks, big colourful ducks almost the size of a small goose, with their young that are so different looking they could almost be another species.

The lagoon at Keyhaven was dotted with avocets, all busy scooping through the mud with their strange upturned bills. I did not expect to see them in summer. They are a crisp black-and-white, long-legged, long-necked and slender, and they seem almost transcendent in their gracefulness. Everything they do is with a seeming refinement and a perfect elegance. They are one of a small handful of birds that no one, surely, could be indifferent to. Some of the flock were this year's young, a little paler, grey and white instead of black and white. After a long absence, the avocet returned to breed in East Anglia after the war, and have slowly spread, so that they are now breeding here on the south coast too.

I walked for many miles along the coast, and then headed back inland, along a long straight track between hedges with fields to either side of me. The sun beat down and the air was thick, and I had finished all the water I had brought with me. It was flying-ant day, and I wondered what the trigger was that made sure they all emerged together. This spectacle may, in truth, occur on more than one day in the year, depending on the vagaries of the weather, but I can tell you that forty-five years ago, in 1974, they all emerged in August too, on 5 August to be precise – my diary tells me so, and it makes me very pleased that my childhood self chose to record this obscure fact for posterity. The narrow track was miles long, and there were discrete clouds of ants every thirty yards or so. It was remarkable how evenly spaced they were; I supposed they must distribute themselves by means of territorial skirmishes. Each cloud was at head height, or perhaps at hedge height, and I couldn't walk around them, so found myself constantly ducking in order to pass beneath them. If this track was three kilometres long, and each colony was thirty metres apart, and each colony contained, I don't know, twenty thousand individuals, there must be something like two million ants living along this single footpath. It seemed extraordinary to think that, had I been here on any other day, I would probably have passed them by completely unnoticed, and yet they were living here in such incredible profusion.

The next time I visit my mother she is sitting in a chair at the window. It is the first time in nearly two months that I have seen her out of her hospital bed. The window looks out to a little copse of trees at the edge of the hospital's staff car park. It is nice to see the trees, she says. I've been looking for birds, but there aren't many, just a few pigeons and crows. I go over and stand at the window, and say: I'll find you something. I am lucky; it only takes a moment. Above the trees, a long-tailed, short-winged bird is circling, circling, and I point it out. My mother asks me what it is. It is a sparrowhawk, in its spring display, a fine sight. So early, once again. Everything seems to be gearing up for a change in season, as the weather has been mild. The problem is that there is almost certain to be a cold snap still to come, that will undo everything. It feels like the seasons can no longer be relied on, that things are no longer in their rightful place.

I return to the coast to make an attempt at a visit that lasts a full day, rather than just a quick hour before darkness falls. This time, the tide is in, so rather than being scattered across the vast expanse of the mudflats, the birds have concentrated around the pools in their thousands. There are parades of geese out on the fields, and occasionally a new skein will swing in, cackling and muttering. Along with the call of the curlews, that is the soundtrack I most instantly recall from my winter visits to the marshes as a child. And there are vast numbers of ducks too, either out on the water or resting at the water's edge. The wigeon and teal are the most numerous, but there are others too: shovelers and tufted ducks, the inevitable mallards, and the graceful pintail, black and white and grey, with a chocolate-brown head and a long, slender tail.

One winter on the marshes as a child, I came upon an injured pintail that was unable to fly, and I caught him, wrapped him in my scarf, and carried him home to care for him. At first he seemed lethargic and a hopeless case, but after a day or two he started to feed, and then he began to tentatively explore the garden, following Fred the chicken about with interest. Every day he seemed to be a little stronger. And then he died. I probably should have sought out expert help, but I'd had some previous success caring for injured wild birds, and I was just a kid.

A kingfisher races along the drainage channel alongside the sea wall in a blur of blue. Little grebes dive in the pools, then bob up like corks, while their handsome cousins the great crested grebes brave the ocean, and a solitary Slavonian grebe too. The avocets are all gathered together on an island in one of the salterns – I count nineteen of them. It is like a fashion parade; they look so elegant. Alone in another smaller pool is a big, white, long-legged bird, wading systematically through the waters and probing the mud, swinging its bill from side to side like a minesweeper. Every time it finds a tasty treat, it throws its head upwards to get the food from beak-tip to throat, as though it were tossing a peanut. It is a spoonbill. It is big and bold, and has what looks like a giant spoon attached to its face. What's not to love?

Later in the day, the birds resting around the pools begin to seem restless; there is something in the air. The tide is beginning to turn, and the mudflats are slowly being exposed, an inch at a time. The first to the feast are clouds of little dunlins. And then the passage begins, as the birds lift off from the salterns and cross the sea wall right above my head, at first tentatively in small groups, and then soon in a great, seemingly endless, torrent of ducks and geese and waders. It is like a twice-daily migration in miniature.

EIGHTEEN

The Reckoning

January 2020

The heaths to the west of Brockenhurst are not flat plains, like those in the far south of the forest, nor are they the steep ridges and valleys of the forest's north. Rather they are intermediate in form, like gently rolling downland, but heather-covered, scattered with pines, with shallow valleys pocketing mires, and streams either grassy-banked or lined with brakes of alder and willow.

Although it was good to have spent time amongst the sheer vitality of the coast, I'm happy to be back in what is more familiar as the forest that I have gradually come to know over the course of the past year. It is a fierce day; there is a biting, piercing wind that sets my eyes streaming and my ears burning. The sheer bleakness is exhilarating. Most of the birds that have not left for the winter have been grounded by the wind, and I seem to have a vast expanse of heathland all to myself. I walk a long circuit, covering miles of ground, beneath a sky that is almost empty of birds. Occasionally, a solitary meadow pipit flushes from beneath my feet, or I spot a fuzz-jack in the gorse. A little handful of redwings blows by; they seem to be having difficulty keeping their course, tossed by the wind. A solitary raven crosses the valley, straight and true.

In a grassy patch sheltered a little by the furze, I come upon a parliament of crows. In general, it is said that if you come upon a congregation of crows, then they are rooks, and if you come upon a solitary rook, then it is a crow. But no, these are carrion crows. Crows generally stick to their pairs and no more, but just occasionally, for inexplicable reasons, inexplicable to me at least, they will gather together in large numbers. Ravens do this too, and magpies; have these occasional mysterious gather-ings. There are crows everywhere, all around me, hopping away cautiously, watching my movements. I would walk past them, leave them in peace, but there is nowhere to go; wherever I look there are more. Suddenly, they all take flight at once, rising from every direction.

There are at least a hundred of them, and they rise above me, tossed every which way by the wind, dancing like the soot from a bonfire, and all calling together. Crowfall.

Finally, I meet someone else who is out and about. Two women, approaching me along the track I am following. They stop and tell me that they too have not seen anyone else in two hours of walking. I note that they are wearing binoculars, and comment that there are not many birds about today. You wouldn't really expect to see much at this time of year, they say. A few redwings and fieldfares, that's all. There is a bit more life in the woods, they tell me, and there was a song thrush singing. That was a good sign.

I walk on in the direction of the woods they have emerged from. Close to the trees I come upon a song thrush scratching on the ground. It lets me come very close before it flies up into a nearby thorn bush and perches at head height. Well then, I say, are you going to give me a song? But it doesn't.

I have heard tell of birdwatchers who have come to the New Forest, seen little, and gone away disappointed. It is certainly not like some bird reserves, which are centred around a single feature such as a lagoon, or a reed bed, or an estuary, that serves as a magnet to all around, enabling the visitor to take a short walk to a hide and have a good prospect of seeing almost everything that the place has to offer. The forest guards its secrets well. Its star attractions are widely dispersed over a large area, and to have a chance of seeing them may take a lot of time and effort. And perhaps luck too. Personally, I like the challenge; to finally get to see something after expending many hours of waiting and watching, and perhaps covering a good deal of ground, makes the eventual moment of success seem that little bit more precious. You feel that you have earned it.

In my childhood memories, the forest is a bright, sunlit place. My visits as a child were almost all in the spring and summer holidays, and my diaries record just the one winter visit in the course of four years. There are some birds that are winter visitors to the forest, such as the great grey shrike that I saw last January, and others that I have yet to see, but the challenge in winter is clearly greater still than it is in the balmy days of summer.

Jotted down in my commonplace book is a list of all my childhood visits: the date, the places visited, and all the observations I saw fit to record at the time. After a year of revisiting the forest it is perhaps now time for a reckoning – of what has changed here since my previous visits almost half a century ago. And also, perhaps, of what has changed in me.

By putting in the time, I have been able to finally catch up on a handful of birds that I missed out on first time around. Birds that I looked out for as a child, but never quite managed to find. Getting to finally spend time with them now feels like a gift to my childhood self. But, of course, there have been losses too. Monitoring of bird populations in Britain has been conducted regularly ever since 1970 – fifty years ago – around the time I first began to seriously watch birds as a boy. Population changes tend to be summarised in terms of their percentage change since 1970. Of course, numerous species of bird may have already been in decline for many years prior to this, but the evidence is not always there. To get an idea of the state of the natural world in earlier times, you must turn to the clues given in older descriptions, such as W. H. Hudson's over a century ago, or Gilbert White writing about the county in pre-industrial times. Both seem to suggest that they were living in a land of plenty when it comes to birds. The

timing of more scientific monitoring of bird populations does usefully mean, however, that the official
baseline for bird numbers matches very closely to my
own personal baseline. What I remember as a child
is the shape of things just as records began to be
systematically kept.

I have already written of the decline in the forest,
alongside much of lowland Britain, of breeding
waders – and this certainly stands out in my childhood
diaries, and very much in my memories too, for these are
striking, charismatic birds. My childhood in the forest
was filled with the cry of the lapwing and the plaintive
trill of the curlew, as well as roding woodcock, and
drumming snipe, and even breeding redshanks yelping
out on the mire. I have felt their absence this past year,
in particular how the loss of these birds seems to have
changed the very soundscape of the heaths. My handful
of sightings this past year felt like little more than an
echo of what once had been.

The group of birds that have largely gone through the
most precipitous decline over the course of the past half-
century are those most associated with farmland.
Looking through my notes from the early seventies, I am

startled in particular by repeated records of two birds I had virtually forgotten about: the turtle dove and the grey partridge. I have not seen either this past year, nor did I really expect to. Since 1970, the population of both has declined by well over ninety per cent; they have almost vanished from the landscape and, sad to say, they have gone so far that they are almost beginning to disappear from memory too, or mine at least.

But for all these changes, the New Forest is still indisputably the same place that I remember from long ago; it looks the same, it smells the same, and most of all it feels just as it does in my memories. Immersing myself in these old haunts of mine has been transportive; it feels like a bridge linking me back to my past. And to some extent coming here to familiar ground has enabled me to look at things anew, and see them almost through the eyes of a child. As we grow older, we tend to become more focused on the bigger picture, on the grand sweep of the landscape, while children take pleasure in immersing themselves in the detail; they see the leaf as well as the tree, and they see the feather on the ground as well as the bird in the air above. I have appreciated, this year, not just restricting my view to the birds and the chequered landscape of rolling heaths and ancient woods, but teaching myself more about the smaller things, the dragonflies and butterflies and flowering plants. It has been an education, in looking closer, in going deeper into the stuff of life. My childhood diaries don't just include lists of birds seen – there are records of lichen species, of fern species, of moths. I feel as though I have won back the healthy obsessions of my youth.

The trail leads me to a bridge across the River Ober. Though it is just a narrow stream here in its upper reaches, it has widened by the bridge to form a substantial shallow pool. Something blue and orange is hovering over the water in a blur, and I stop on the bridge to watch it. A kingfisher. They most often perch on overhanging branches and fish from there, but here there is no suitable vegetation, so it is making do. I have had a couple of fleeting views of kingfishers this year, but this is my closest and most protracted sighting so far, as it hovers almost like a kestrel over the pool, its body and head still but its wings moving almost too fast to see. It is perhaps overdue; I remember long, vivid observations here in the forest during my childhood visits. In 1974, a little way downstream on this very same watercourse, I came upon a nesting site, and sitting on the opposite bank, watched enchanted as the pair hurtled in and out of their burrow. This bird suddenly drops into the water, with a plink like that from a tossed stone, and emerges a moment later, victoriously holding a fish that is barely even an inch long. It carries it to a waterside hawthorn, and eats its tiny catch. I watch until it has completed its meal, when it launches forward, turns on a pin, and zooms away downstream in a blue blur.

NINETEEN

Migrants in Flight

January 2020

It is not very often these days that I fly anywhere; it begins to feel less and less justifiable as we become increasingly aware of the consequences to the environment. To be fair, even in my globe-trotting youth, I travelled overland as much as I possibly could. It felt to me that I got a much better sense of where I was in the world, of the distances I had covered, rather than just stepping into an airport in one place, and emerging a few hours later somewhere wildly different. But on the spur of the moment, I have grabbed at an opportunity that has led me thousands of miles from my home shores.

For the past two months while my mother has been in hospital, I have fallen behind rather with my writing. My visits to the forest have been less frequent, and I have struggled to find the time to write up my notes. But now my mother is much better, and has finally been able to return home, and I have the chance to play catch-up. My old friend Vivenie told me she was heading to Rwanda for a short visit, to see family and to discuss business, and invited me to tag along. I could stay in the properties of various of her relatives, scattered around the country, use them as writing retreats, she said. I have long been promising to make a return visit; I was last here fifteen years ago on a short working trip, making a film that related to the genocide of the Tutsi. It was all work and no play, and I didn't even have a chance to leave the capital. I vowed then that I would return one day to see more of what the country has to offer.

My friend Viv has her own history of a house on fire: when she was still a teenager, a mob had come to her house, looted it, and burnt it to the ground. They had come with the intention of killing her and her entire family, and were driven incandescent with rage to find that they had all already managed to flee and go into hiding. It rather puts my own brush with fire into perspective.

A few days after my arrival, I am sitting on a jetty

stretching out into a lake surrounded by steep hillsides, and there are kingfishers all around. There is a pair perched to the left of me, a pair to the right, and more out hovering over the water, diving repeatedly, plinking into it just like that kingfisher at Ober Water only a few days ago. This lake must be stuffed with tiny fish. Indeed, I can see them shoaling in the clear shallows. These kingfishers are very different, however, from the ones back home. They are much bigger, and black and white: African pied kingfishers. There are also a few examples of a kingfisher much more like our native variety, and more inclined to dive from a low perch. The malachite kingfisher is tiny, noticeably smaller than our own, which is already small enough to surprise most people who see one for the first time. While our kingfisher is turquoise and electric blue, the malachite is a deep cobalt blue, so dark it is almost purple. And it has a dispro-portionately huge, brilliant red bill, so that as it flies low across the water it looks like nothing so much as a beak with wings.

The other places I have stayed in so far during the course of my visit have been well equipped, but here I am back to basics, which perhaps suits me better, or at least my idea of myself. This village, such as it is, is no more than a loose aggregation of mud huts close to the lakeside, along a rutted red dirt road that extends for fifty kilometres along the northern shore of Lake Muhazi. I could never have found this place unaided; my friends have dropped me here and headed back to Kigali. The villagers are friendly, but we have no common language, and they are no doubt somewhat perplexed by my presence among them, and why I might want to be there. To be honest, I'm not sure I could explain it to them even if I did speak the language. The hut in which I am staying is like a monastic cell – about eight foot square, and containing nothing whatsoever apart from a sleeping mat and a house gecko that is doing a poor job of keeping down the mosquitoes. There is no water in the village save for what comes from the lake, and no shops. Just a couple of the huts have an electricity supply; these serve as bars, and each night people gather around them, drinking banana beer and listening to music. It is a twenty-four-hour village; by the time the last drinkers retire at dawn, there are already people out working their crops, and the children are heading off for the long walk to school.

My hut – or rather, I should say, the hut in which I have been kindly invited to stay – has a tin roof, and spending time inside during the day is not realistic. It becomes unbearably hot. And so I find myself sitting on a jetty over the water, attempting to write. But it is not so easy to write when you are surrounded by birds. It seems that every half-hour I see something new, another species of sunbird or weaver or bee-eater, or a circling bird of prey. And as night falls and the birds settle, I am buzzed by little grey-faced bats. It seems extraordinary that such a small, mountainous, landlocked country, a country just one third the size of Scotland, should have a bird list far exceeding that of the whole of Britain. There are at least sixty species of birds of prey alone, and I have easily spotted twenty already, without going anywhere near a national park: long-crested eagles and tawny eagles, augur buzzards and mountain buzzards, African goshawks and dark chanting-goshawks, small sparrow-hawks and grey kestrels, African harrier-hawks, and many more.

This is the most densely populated country in Africa; not that it has any substantially sized cities beyond the capital. Rather, it is a rural economy, a nation of smallholders. The population density of Rwanda is almost exactly the same as the population density of England. Other parts of the UK obviously have lower populations; divided up equally between us all, we would get an acre each. Imagine what it would look like if we all claimed our acre and farmed it as an allotment; that is pretty much what Rwanda looks like, but they have better weather. Yet of course in Britain there are individuals who own the acres of the entire population of a sizeable city.

Looking across the lake, what I see is the characteristic view of Rwanda: high hills falling steeply down to the water, the hillsides roughly terraced over the course of centuries. Fertile soil, rich and volcanic, with a decent amount of rainfall. The hillsides are dotted with huts seemingly at random, occasionally forming a small cluster that will pass for a village. Everybody owns a small plot. There will always be bananas and corn. There may be a small young wood for charcoal burning. There may be a bed of potatoes or onions, or cassava or beans, perhaps a few fruit trees with a couple of goats tethered beneath them, mangoes or oranges or tree tomatoes. This is a subsistence-plus economy: everything you need to feed your family, plus a little to spare for market. The hillsides form a lush patchwork quilt of different shades of green. There are some parts of the country that have been turned over to cash crops, mostly tea and coffee plantations, and there are areas where the last remaining fragments of Rift Valley rainforest have been preserved before they are all lost, and the rainforest specialists with them, but the vast majority of the country looks pretty much like this: a million tiny farms, and not a fence in sight.

When I walk along the convoluted trails that wind between the different plots, the most striking thing is that the landscape is heaving with life; buzzing with insects, scampered over by lizards, and with a bird in every bush. It is the sheer untidiness of agriculture here – variety breeds variety. It is the opposite of a prairie or a cattle ranch, where you have vast expanses devoted to a single species, with the rest kept at bay with pesticides and weedkillers. It helps to reinforce my notion that human occupation and use of the land need not be harmful to life, that rather the sacrifice of the earth that turns agricultural land into wasteland is the product of a broken system, one which encourages the consolidation of land into the hands of progressively fewer and fewer people.

I woke early this morning, while the waters of the lake were still pink, and took a long walk along the dirt road that followed the shoreline. I wanted to get a few miles in before the heat became too much for me. The days get hotter and hotter as they wear on, but it is the rainy season, so some days the heat will build to thunder, and then a flash downpour that will finally begin to bring the temperature back down a little, only to start building again. There was plenty of foot traffic; people would do a double-take when they saw me, and then look delighted when I acknowledged them, perhaps trying out the few words they knew in French or English. Bicycles went past laden with bananas or sacks of onions, and any rider of an unladen bicycle would stop to offer me a backy. Walking for pleasure was perhaps not in their repertoire. I dawdled, my attention caught every few minutes by a new bird or plant, or a fresh perspective on the lake. Many of the birds I was able to have a stab at identifying, while some continued to elude me. A fiscal flew down and plucked a tiny snake from the road-bed, then flew up into a nearby tree and began to bash it on a branch. The fiscal is a type of black-and-white shrike; it reminded me of the great grey shrike that I had seen in the forest last winter.

Most of the birds here are very different from our own, with whole families that are not represented in the temperate north. But not all of them. Though the lake was being skimmed by African swallows too, the most numerous were our own swallows. Not just our own species, but the same actual birds, migrated here for the winter. They helped to make me feel surprisingly at home in such an unfamiliar environment, as though I had come all this way in company, all migrants together.

A falcon came swinging in, fast and rangy and long-winged. It looped above my head, then settled on the topmost twig of a small roadside tree right beside me and began to preen. It was only a bloody hobby, the bird I have been looking out for to no avail all year in the New Forest. I stopped and admired it; it was a beautiful little creature, sleek and black-capped and alert. It was here on its annual migration of course; follow the swallow. This is where it comes to during our winter. Another thing about the birds here, even the ones that have come from home – they seem less nervous in the presence of a human observer, more relaxed, less flighty. Perhaps it is because we are outside the breeding season and they have fewer worries. They are on their holidays too. Or perhaps they are less subject to persecution here. The bird stayed long, upright on its vertical twig. I began to wonder if its patience would outlast mine. I hated the thought that I might end up having to just walk away and leave it, for who knew when I might get to see one again; conceivably never. But finally, and without warning, it sprang, and as it did so, a second bird emerged from within the heart of the tree. I could scarcely believe that all this time there had been a second hobby there, hidden from view. The two falcons, with their long, scimitar wings tip to tip, almost danced in the air together. The bird had looked tiny on its treetop perch, but as it suddenly unfurled the crescent moon of its wings and launched, it seemed to suddenly expand to fill the available space. The two birds spun together like giant swifts circling a tower, surely the most graceful in flight of any bird.

TWENTY

Whistling in the Wind

February 2020

This is by far the largest flock of redwings I have seen here this winter. There must be over a thousand of them. Perhaps they are beginning to gather in preparation for their long journey north once again. They all face the same way, head down into the wind, and the birds at the rear are constantly flying low over the heads of the others and taking their place at the very front of the flock. In this way, it looks as though the whole troupe are in constant rolling motion, cartwheeling their way over the heath. Starlings will work a field in this same way, ensuring that no single individual misses out on the richest pickings.

A kestrel is hovering above the heath, fighting against the wind to hold its place. And then a sudden gust snatches it away, and it peels off and is dashed into the distance at an almost inconceivable speed. Then I see a second falcon, flying low and fast above the heather tops. It rises and falls, its wings flickering at speed, twisting and turning, racing the wind. It is grey-backed and tiny in comparison to the kestrel. This is a merlin, a little male, barely bigger than a thrush, a bird of the uplands, here on a winter visit from the northern moors or perhaps even further afield. It is wild out here again today, and these birds seem to be rejoicing in it. A little later, on another heath, I see a different, much larger, bird of prey: a hen harrier, blowing by. I had been looking out for one ever since I had seen the merlin, as for all their differences, they frequently seem to come together, and will often appear in the same place at the same time. Both nest on the high moors, but in the winter when the moors are almost bereft of life they will come down to the coast and the lowland heaths. I have been vaguely looking out for them all winter; it seems perfect that I should finally see both on the same day.

My planned year of visits to the forest has come to an end, but I find myself back here again anyway. It feels as though coming to the forest has become part of my routine now; I imagine that I shall keep on returning for as long as I am able, and for as long as I find myself living within easy reach. This forest has become a significant part of my life; perhaps it always was, and I was just not allowing myself to remember.

While I was out on the heath, a fierce wind blew every last thought out of my head, but here within the shelter of the woods, it is relatively calm and peaceful. A weak, wintry sun shines from between the scudding clouds, and I sit on a fallen trunk to rest. It is quiet here, just the occasional brief fizz of birdsong from somewhere in the trees that I cannot quite identify; I was never much good at birdsong. Probably robins; robins set up winter territories and almost never stop their singing. There has been much rain, and the track through the woods has been churned into deep mud by the hooves of passing ponies. Out beyond the woodland edge, the grassy flatlands have turned into a water world. The rivers have burst their banks and fanned out across the lawns; any route over is criss-crossed by sudden streams and fleeting shallow pools that reflect the clouds above. It is as if earth, sky and water have blurred their boundaries and begun to merge.

It is a well-established fact that time spent in nature is good for body and soul. Scientific studies have shown that even a couple of hours a week is enough to make a difference, to improve mental health, to reduce the likelihood of many serious physical health conditions, to aid recovery. I can feel this in my bones; I breathe more easily here in the quiet of the woods. As I sit on my trunk, it is as though a weight is lifted off my shoulders, and I am at peace with myself, secure in my place in the world. Perhaps this is why I feel so disgruntled that so much of the countryside is fenced off from me; it is as though I am being told I am no longer welcome in the place that I feel I most belong. I should say that the weight on my shoulders is not a heavy burden; it has never been in my nature to feel that the load of life is unsupportable. But perhaps that itself is because I have led a largely outdoor existence.

There are whole books exploring the restorative powers of nature. There is a wealth of memoirs, by people who have been broken by life's cruelties, worn down by trauma, who have found some level of redemption by spending time out in the natural world. Many of these books can be very moving and beautiful, and can help teach us why we should value the world around us, and not let it go to waste. And yet it is important to recognise, too, that our relationship with the natural world is a reciprocal one; there has to be give as well as take.

There is a danger that we begin to only see nature in transactional terms: we value it because of what it can do for us. We need also to think, not just about what nature offers us, but what we can offer nature. We need to think more collaboratively about the non-human world, for we are all in this together, all occupying the same limited space. There is a branch of environmental science that tries to put an economic value on the contribution of nature in terms of ecosystem services. We should save the bees because they contribute a hundred and fifty billion pounds a year to the world economy by means of pollination services. I can just about begin to see the reasoning behind this, for perhaps a spreadsheet filled with numbers is the only language with which we can speak to politicians and businessmen. This attempt to count the price of the world includes a figure for recreation services. What is the price of my walk in the woods? Can it be quantified, because it helps keep me sane enough to work, and therefore to pay taxes? I'm sorry, but this seems like a miserable way to look at the world.

As a writer who loves nature, it would come very naturally to me to just walk through the woods, take joy in the animals and plants that I come upon, and depict them as creatively as I can, along with the many small epiphanies that they bring me. There is some value in this. As Rachel Carson, author of *Silent Spring*, put it: focusing our attention on the wonders of the world around us is incompatible with an appetite for destruction. But it no longer feels that purely observational writing is enough. The time has gone when I could even write a private nature diary, just for myself, and turn a blind eye to the wider implications of what I see. To delight in an encounter with a rare and beautiful bird, while wilfully ignoring why it is rare, why it is threatened, is itself a deeply political choice, and one which no longer feels supportable. And, really, nothing is more political than the way we engage with the world around us. We have an obligation to see the world for what it is, the bad as well as the good, and we have to blinker ourselves to keep on pretending that it is not broken.

Many early nature writers were landed gentry, the only people who had the necessary combination of access to land, leisure and literacy. Some of these writers were very capable and knowledgeable, and their passion for the wildlife they depicted is indisputable. But they often demonstrated a very particular perspective, with a sense of: This is my land, and here are its glories. Things are gradually beginning to change, and we are starting to hear a wider range of points of view. Many of the finest works of nature writing in recent years have been written by women, and we are just beginning to see the publication of what feels like a first wave of nature writing by black and minority writers. But there is still a long way to go. It is hard to break free of some of the assumptions of such a long tradition. We need to hear from the outsider as well as the insider, we need the view from the council estate as well as the country estate, we need the perspective of the migrant, the landless and the dispossessed.

Nature writing may often be read for comfort and reassurance, but perhaps we need to allow a little room for anger too, for the ability to rage at everything that has been taken from us, and been taken by us. We may want to be told that all is well with the world. We may want to believe that though the tribulations of the world can grind us down, the wonders of nature are still all around us, ready to restore us to a state of equanimity. But the natural world is in a state of crisis. It is reasonable to fret about this, and think about changes we could make to our lifestyles that might help: we could eat less meat; we could fly less, drive less, consume less; we could use less plastic; we could plant some trees. I have done all these things myself, to a greater or lesser extent. But I can't help but feel that I have been conned, that we have all been conned, into believing that we all share equal responsibility, that it's down to our own individual selfishness, our own lifetime of bad choices. In truth, we have all been dropped into a system that was never of our own choosing. A system that is designed and maintained by a minuscule proportion of the world's population, the people who have stolen the world from us, the landowners and politicians and major corporations.

The world is not in trouble because we make lazy choices and are irresponsible consumers; it is in trouble because of those who have grabbed at the fortunes to be made by ripping fossil fuels out of the earth, turning surpluses into plastics, promoting needs where none previously existed. We live in a society in which the bad choices have been embedded into every aspect of our daily lives, and the people who are actually most able to make a difference seem to be the ones who are least willing to try. I am sure that they will tell themselves that they are no different from anyone else, that anyone would do the same, given the chance, and that life is a zero-sum game in which they are just the best players. They may perhaps feel trapped within the same system as the rest of us, but as its principal beneficiaries they have a vested interest in keeping things just as they are. I refuse to accept that it is simply down to human nature; it is my hope that most people just want a decent life, and know when to say enough is enough. I cannot believe that untrammelled greed is a quality intrinsic to all of us, just waiting for the opportunity to flourish. And, ultimately, I would contest that the absurd luxuries that people may strive for, the desire of some people to possess more of the world around them than anyone else, is just smoke and mirrors in any case. Nobody can really, truly, own anything, save perhaps for the thoughts in their head. It is merely a convention that we have been talked into abiding by, for fear of losing what little we may like to imagine is ours. We belong to the world; the world does not belong to us.

I am not saying that we should just give up, and say: I didn't create this mess, how could I possibly help fix it? Shrugging our shoulders and absolving ourselves of any obligation to even pretend to care is surely the worst option of all. Rather, we have to keep believing, perhaps in the face of the evidence all around us, that if a sufficiently large number of us raise our voices, and are prepared to change our way of living accordingly, then perhaps, just perhaps, the people who actually hold the power to make a difference may be forced to sit up and listen.

It may seem that I am whistling in the wind; that I should accept the way of the world, and that the only way forward is to be pragmatic, to tweak the existing system, to adopt incremental changes that will lead us gradually in the right direction, one small step at a time, which may be enough to hold back the flood. My position may seem to be an extreme one. But I would argue that the situation in which we find ourselves, that we are told to accept as inevitable, is itself one of ludicrous extremity.

On the one side, we have the rights of that incredibly tiny proportion of the world's population who have all the wealth to maintain their profit margins; on the other, we also hold the future well-being of the vast majority of life on earth. What could be more extreme than that? I have to believe that this is not what people want, and it cannot continue to be the future, if we are to have a future.

I sit on my fallen trunk in the woods and wonder where I shall go today. I am without ambition. When I first started revisiting the forest over a year ago, I did not set myself particular targets, but I suppose I did have some hopes, that I would encounter some of the key species of plants and animals that the forest has to offer. And I feel that I have achieved this, far beyond any expectations that I may have had; if I see nothing further today, I will still not go away disappointed. I am satisfied with my year in that regard; I feel that I have been lucky. Or perhaps it has not been luck, and nor has it been skill – rather it has simply been a matter of putting in the time. Over the course of the past year I have visited the forest about thirty times in total. And yet I know that I have only touched the surface; on reflection I can see that this is clearly demonstrated by just how many creatures I have seen only once in all my many visits. So many solitary sightings. I know for sure that, no matter how many times I came here, I would never run out of new experiences.

It has been a year of wonders, my forest year. I have had the opportunity to experience so much that I had never anticipated; great clouds of spiralling butterflies, a sea of orchids, flowers that I had never even known existed, and sudden, unexpected sightings of creatures of great beauty. A nightjar watching over me as darkness fell, falcons on the wing, hawks and honey buzzards deep in the woods. I have listened to the cackle of the geese on the marshes, and the aching trill of the last curlews. I have heard the woodlark sing, for all its lost chords, and the comforting call of the raven, back at last. The year has been thick with scents, heather and furze and bog myrtle, peat and pine and the sour smell of boots full of bog water. These things give life new meaning.

In these visits I have indulged my memories, and have revisited virtually all the places I remember from my childhood. Lately I have rather found myself revisiting places that I first saw earlier in the year, perhaps with a little diversion for the sake of novelty. It is like a kind of rolling nostalgia. It has been a year of reflection, and I feel that I know myself better than when I began, and understand more clearly the way the world could be, and ought to be. This wind-blasted wood is peaceful, perhaps not truly wild but beautiful nonetheless. I don't want to lose this. I feel very much at home here, not because I feel any sense of ownership or personal entitlement, but rather precisely because I don't. Not because I feel that this land is mine but because I feel that this land is everybody's, and nobody's. I know that I am free to wander about wherever I will, I know that no one will approach me to ask what the hell I think I'm doing. No one can challenge my right to be here, and that is enough – that is all I ask for.

The birds are quiet; for a long time I see nothing but the faithful, the blackbirds and robins that are always the most visible here in winter. The blackbirds scratching about among the leaf litter, occasionally taking flight in alarm at what appears to be nothing, and the robins hopping about close by and keeping watch over me. And then, finally, a mixed flock of tits come by, and with them a solitary treecreeper, and a little further off, a great spotted woodpecker, watching them all as if curious.

I step out of the woods and join a trail that winds along the woodland edge, past wood pasture, past oakwood and beechwood and a plantation of pines, all to my right, while the heath stretches out into the distance to my left. There is nobody else about; I imagine it is too muddy for most. I splash my way along, leaping over tiny streams that have sprung up overnight. There has been a lot of wind and rain this year, and especially this winter, but really it has been another lost winter; there has been no snow and not even many nights of frost, at least here in the south. Birds singing and bats flying in December, as if confused, as if the seasons are losing their meaning, or the meaning they once had.

As I walk alongside a fine stand of beech trees, a bird flies up from the ground and into the branches above, and then another, then two, then five, and then a whole stream of them, as if they are pouring out of the ground. Redwings. On the ground, amongst the leaf litter, they are completely invisible to me; it is not until they are on the wing that I can discern their presence. It is as if they are materialising before my eyes. Just as the stream of redwings is beginning to slow to a trickle, they are followed by smaller birds, a great flock of them. Black and white with a fine tinge of orange; bramblings, another winter visitor from the far north. Between the two species there must be many hundreds of birds in the flock, and yet if they had not flushed, I could easily have walked right past them and not noticed a thing.

I walk on and I walk long, through woods and across heaths and mires, passing pools that are filled with the reflections of trees and clouds. I walk in peace. Following an animal track through fallen bracken I come upon a roe buck sleeping in a hollow. It has fine small antlers, still partway through its new growth for the year. It senses me and jumps to its feet, and bounds away, its white rump bobbing. It is determined to put some distance between us, but it is not panicked. When it reaches the edge of the nearest woods, it stops and turns, and watches me. There is a familiar call; a raven cronking. I look around, and finally see it right above my head; it has crept up on me from behind. I look around to search for a second bird that it is calling to, but it seems to be alone. It flips over onto its back, right above me, flies upside down for a moment. This is one of their favourite tricks. It calls again. Perhaps it is calling to me, perhaps it is saying: I see you.

I have not walked this way before. In a dip on the heath I come upon a hidden mire, unmarked on my map, fringed with alders and sallow, and with the skeleton of a drowned tree in its centre. Everything is rust red: the fallen bracken, the reeds and sedges, even the water itself. A long pool stretches to left and right as far as I can see, dotted with little reedy islands, while the copse of pines on the horizon that I have been heading towards remains tantalisingly out of reach. I begin to wade across, but can soon tell that it will be too deep; not the water, but the soft mud beneath it. I am going to have to walk the long way round, but which way, left or right? I conclude that it doesn't really matter; it will add significantly to my journey whichever way I choose, but I will get there in the end. I decide on right, for no reason at all. The combination of grass and heather all around the mire is sodden, and squelches and slurps beneath my feet, but it is springy too, and I find myself bouncing across the heath, skipping from tussock to tussock, in search of anything that could resemble a trail.

There is a sudden gust of wind that sends a shimmer

racing over the pool from end to end at great speed, shattering the reflection of the sky into thousands of tiny pieces. As if an angel has just passed over the face of the waters. And then the first drops of rain start to fall. The sky is darkening. A storm is coming. I pause beside a furze brake and race to put on my rain gear; this is going to be more than a shower.

The wind has no direction; it blows back and forth, from left and right, from front and back. The long view across the heath is blurred, as through the condensation on a window. The wall of conifers at the far edge of the heath is fading from view, becoming just a smudge in the distance. Rain falls all across the land. It falls on the open ocean, where the winds send breakers crashing against our shores. It falls on heath and farm. It falls on wildwood and plantation. It falls on town and country. It falls on river and stream, and sends them swelling beyond their banks. It falls on ancient oak and beech, and it falls on the dripping pines. It falls relentlessly, indiscriminately. It falls on the ponies hiding among the flowering gorse, and it falls on the roe buck sheltering in the woods. It falls on the birds in their hidden retreats. It falls on commoner and wanderer, it falls on peasant and landowner, without distinction. A world of water. The horizon fades from view; there is no horizon, just water and wind. Everything becomes one.

Further Reading

Carson, Rachel, *Silent Spring* (Boston, 1962)

Clare, John, *Poems Descriptive of Rural Life* (London, 1820)

Cobbett, William, *Rural Rides* (London, 1830)

Deakin, Roger, *Wildwood: A Journey Through Trees* (London, 2007)

Frohawk, Frederick William, *Natural History of British Butterflies* (London, 1924)

Hudson, William Henry, *Hampshire Days* (London, 1903)

Leopold, Aldo, *A Sand County Almanac* (New York, 1949)

Macdonald Lockhart, James, *Raptor: A Journey Through Birds* (London, 2016)

Matsuo, Bashō, *Oi no Kobumi (The Records of a Travel-Worn Satchel)* (Edo, 1688)

Monbiot, George, *Feral: Searching for Enchantment on the Frontiers of Rewilding* (London, 2013)

Mooallem, Jon, *Wild Ones: A Sometimes Dismaying, Weirdly Reassuring Story About Looking at People Looking at Animals in America* (New York/London, 2013)

Shoard, Marion, *The Theft of the Countryside* (London, 1981)

— *This Land is Our Land* (London, 1987)

Shrubsole, Guy, *Who Owns England? How We Lost Our Green and Pleasant Land and How to Take it Back* (London, 2019)

Smith, Len, *Romany Nevi Wesh: An Informal History of the New Forest Gypsies* (Lyndhurst, 2004)

Tree, Isabella, *Wilding: The Return of Nature to a British Farm* (London, 2018)

Tubbs, Colin R., *The New Forest: A Natural History* (London, 1986)

Wall Kimmerer, Robin, *Braiding Sweetgrass: Indigenous Wisdom, Scientific Knowledge, and the Teachings of Plants* (Minneapolis, 2013)

White, Gilbert, *The Natural History and Antiquities of Selborne* (London, 1789)

Wise, John R., *The New Forest: Its History and Its Scenery* (London, 1863)

You are invited to join us behind the scenes at Tinder Press

TINDER PRESS

To meet our authors, browse our books
and discover exclusive content on our
blog visit us at

www.tinderpress.co.uk

For the latest news and views from the team
Follow us on Twitter

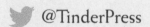 @TinderPress

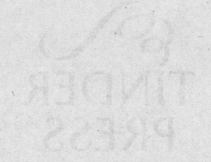